SCIENTIFIC BREAKTHROUGHS

Chemistry, Earth, and Space Sciences

TEACHER RESOURCES

Edited by Tim Cooke

LIGHTBOX
openlightbox.com

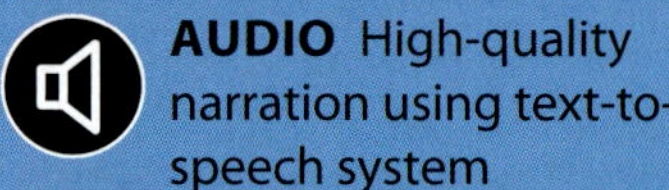

Lightbox is an all-inclusive digital solution for the teaching and learning of curriculum topics in an original, groundbreaking way. Lightbox is based on National Curriculum Standards.

STANDARD FEATURES OF LIGHTBOX

AUDIO High-quality narration using text-to-speech system

WEBLINKS Curated links to external, child-safe resources

INTERACTIVE MAPS Interactive maps and aerial satellite imagery

VIDEOS Embedded high-definition video clips

SLIDESHOWS Pictorial overviews of key concepts

QUIZZES Ten multiple choice questions that are automatically graded and emailed for teacher assessment

ACTIVITIES Printable PDFs that can be emailed and graded

TRANSPARENCIES Step-by-step layering of maps, diagrams, charts, and timelines

KEY WORDS Matching key concepts to their definitions

MORE Extra information and details on the subject

FIRST HAND Letters, diaries, and other primary sources

DOCS Speeches, newspaper articles, and other historical documents

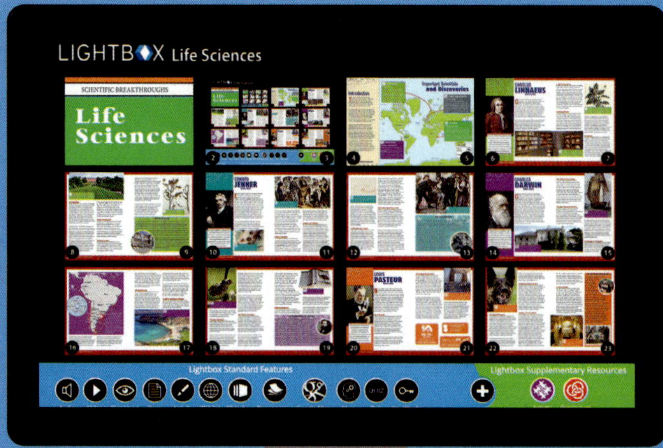

Contents

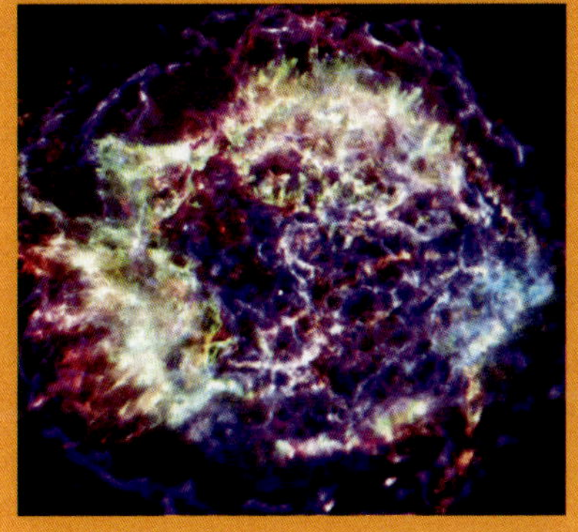

RUBRIC

Conducting an Interview

Students will conduct an interview with a member of the scientific community about a significant discovery he or she made or important research he or she conducted. The student is to submit an audio recording and transcript of the interview. An exemplary interview will meet the following criteria.

- Clearly defines the purpose of the interview
- Conducts thorough background research to inform the focus of the interview and the questions
- Drafts a complete list of thoughtful, in-depth, and varied questions prior to the interview
- Interviews a subject with relevant knowledge on the topic and time period in question
- Asks questions in a logical order, building upon each other
- Treats the interview subject in a polite and professional manner
- Does not interrupt or rush the interview subject
- Shows interest and enthusiasm in responses and follow-up questions
- Chooses follow-up questions that demonstrate active listening
- Asks for clarification and further details when necessary
- Asks questions about personal experiences related to the topic
- Asks questions regarding factual information and the interview subject's opinion on the topic
- Asks creative questions that reflect fresh insights on the topic
- Records the full interview in a quiet environment
- Organizes and edits the interview transcript to be clear and factual

Introduction

Ancient peoples looked up to the sky and assumed that Earth was at the center and the stars and planets orbited around it. In the Middle Ages, the same view was taught by the Catholic Church. It was not until the 1500s that the Polish **astronomer** Nicolaus Copernicus demonstrated scientifically that this was not the case. Early the next century, Galileo Galilei used the newly invented telescope to make more discoveries about space. His work led to a better understanding of the **solar system**. It was only in the 1900s, however, that astronomers began to get a true idea of the vastness of space. Space is full of **galaxies** with billions of stars, and Earth is just one of many billions of planets. Meanwhile, the processes that change the face of Earth itself were understood for the first time in the mid-1900s.

While some scientists studied the heavens, others learned more about the building blocks of the universe. In the 1700s, they began to investigate the nature of air. This led to the discovery of **elements**, the fundamental substances that make up the universe. Studying the elements led to a deeper understanding of **atoms** and even tinier particles. In turn, this proved to offer clues about the creation of the universe and its eventual fate.

Edwin Hubble

Mount Wilson, California, United States

Using the largest telescope in the world at the time, U.S. astronomer Edwin Hubble realized in 1923 that faint "stars" were distant galaxies. Each galaxy held billions of stars. Not only did Hubble discover that the universe was far bigger than previously thought, he also realized that it was getting bigger all the time.

Alexander von Humboldt

Quito, Ecuador

Alexander von Humboldt explored South America in the early 1800s. His observations there led him to come up with the idea that plants and animals live in systems. This gave rise to the idea of ecosystems, which are at the heart of the study of natural history today.

Important Scientists and Discoveries

Dmitri Mendeleev

St. Petersburg, Russia

The chemist Dmitri Mendeleev was considering a way to group elements for a textbook he was writing, when he was struck by the idea that they could be grouped into regular "periods." The groups were based upon the elements' **atomic weight**. Mendeleev arranged the known elements into a **periodic table**. He left gaps where he correctly predicted new elements would later be discovered.

Nicolaus Copernicus

Frombork, Poland

The Polish astronomer Nicolaus Copernicus believed that ancient accounts of the heavens did not agree with what astronomers saw in the night sky. He used observation and **mathematics** to produce his theory that Earth circled the Sun, not the other way around. The theory was controversial, and it was only published at the end of Copernicus's life.

MAP LEGEND

- Featured location
- Land
- Water

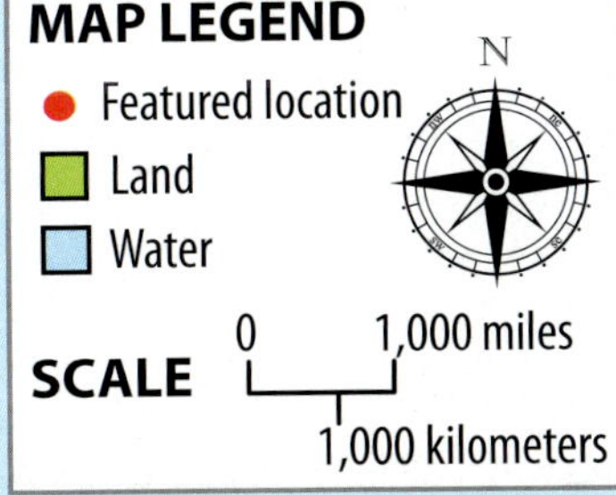

SCALE 0 — 1,000 miles / 1,000 kilometers

EXTENSION ACTIVITY

Google Maps

Important Scientists and Discoveries

Explore these locations using street view to learn more about important scientists and their discoveries.

1. What do these locations have in common with each other? What are the differences between them?
2. Why are these discoveries associated with these specific locations? In your opinion, would the work of these scientists and their discoveries have been possible elsewhere? Support your opinions with examples.

NICOLAUS COPERNICUS

1473–1543

Copernicus founded modern astronomy. He challenged the ancient belief that Earth was at the center of the universe. His theories brought him into conflict with church leaders, however.

Nicolaus Copernicus was born in 1473 in Torún, Poland. He studied at the University of Kraków, and then spent about 10 years in Italy. There, he studied philosophy, mathematics, and astronomy. He also qualified as a lawyer specializing in Church law and as a physician. Back in Poland, Copernicus served as secretary to a bishop before moving to Frauenburg in East Prussia, where he was appointed a canon of the cathedral. This post allowed him ample time to pursue his study of astronomy.

The ancient Greek astronomer Ptolemy described his theories on the movement of the Sun, Moon, and stars in his work, *Amalgest* (150 AD). Copernicus challenged these theories.

Challenging the Ptolemaic System

In the fourth century BC, Greek philosopher Aristotle described a universe in which transparent spheres carried heavenly bodies in circular **orbits** around an immobile Earth. Astronomers could see that the Sun, Moon, and planets did not actually move this way, however. The Greek Ptolemy suggested that, while Earth remained at the center of a planet's orbit, the planet moved in another cycle, called an epicycle, centered on its own orbit, or "deferent."

There were reasons for accepting Ptolemy's view. The Sun does seem to move across the sky each day. Astronomers also reasoned that Earth could not rotate on its own axis, because buildings would collapse or people would feel a rush of wind against their faces. A third argument was that Christian thinkers in the Middle Ages thought the Sun moved at God's will.

A New Approach

Copernicus saw a number of problems with the Ptolemaic system. He was in favor of a simpler system, in which bodies moved in a uniform circular motion around a single point. In about 1510, he began to share the view of Aristarchus of Samos and other Greek thinkers that Earth circles the Sun. In other words, he thought the universe is "heliostatic," from the Greek meaning "stationary Sun." In his book, *On the Revolutions of the* ***Celestial*** *Spheres,* Copernicus argued that, whether it is Earth or the heavens that are moving, the results are the same to an observer. The stars still seem to revolve.

Copernicus decided that the planets, including Earth, moved around the Sun, and that the Moon revolved around Earth. He believed that this would explain more simply why the other

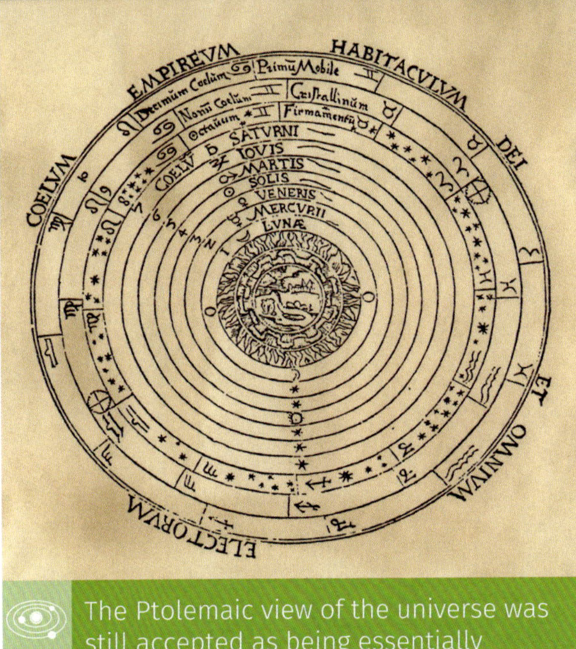

The Ptolemaic view of the universe was still accepted as being essentially correct during Copernicus's lifetime, around a thousand years after it was created.

planets moved in the way they did, and why there was a variation in the brightness of the planets. Copernicus was even able to place the five known planets in order from the Sun. Mercury was nearest, then Venus, Earth, Mars, Jupiter, and Saturn. Copernicus also argued, like some earlier Greek astronomers, that Earth spins, or rotates, daily on its axis. However, Copernicus continued to accept Aristotle's idea that there were eight transparent spheres carrying the known planets, the Sun, the Moon, and the stars, and that the planets moved in a perfect circular motion.

Arguments with the Church

Copernicus completed *On the Revolutions of the Celestial Spheres* in 1514, but did not publish it until 1543. It is possible that he was concerned about the reaction of the Church. At this time, the Catholic Church was extremely powerful. There appeared to be some risks for Copernicus if he published his theory, because it contradicted a Biblical text.

EXTENSION ACTIVITY

More

Ptolemy

Review the most important works of Ptolemy.

1. How did the scientific approach of Ptolemy differ from that of modern scientists? Create an evidence-based logical response.
2. Why might the Ptolemaic system still have been accepted in Copernicus's times? Which system would you have followed? Why?

Weblink

Ptolemy versus Copernicus

Compare and contrast the theories of Ptolemy and Copernicus.

1. Why was Copernicus's theory criticized both "on theological and philosophical grounds"? What did Osiander write in his preface to Copernicus's *De Revolutionibus Orbium Coelestium* to minimize the potential for controversy?
2. How did Kepler and Tycho Brahe improve Copernicus's theory? Explain the differences between the theories of Copernicus, Kepler, and Brahe in your own words.

RUBRIC

Analyzing a Primary Source

Students will complete a thorough analysis of a primary source. An exemplary analysis will meet the following criteria.

- Identifies the creator of the source
- Explains what medium was used to create the primary source
- Describes why the source qualifies as a primary one
- Explores any literary devices used in the source
- Identifies the intended audience for the source
- Relates the creator's goals in creating the source
- Illustrates knowledge of the period and location in which the source was created
- Distinguishes between facts and opinions found in the source
- Examines the reliability of the source's creator
- Compares the source with similar documents
- Cites additional sources used in the analysis
- Presents information in a clear, concise manner
- Uses correct spelling, grammar, and punctuation

In a heliocentric, or Sun-centered, universe, Earth spins as it orbits the Sun, creating the periods of day and night around the globe.

According to the Bible, humankind was at the very heart of God's creation. Now, Copernicus suggested that the place where humans lived was not at the center of the universe at all. Many years later, in 1633, the Italian astronomer Galileo Galilei experienced the Church's anger. He was put on trial for supporting Copernicus's theory.

It was the Protestant reformer Martin Luther who seemed most horrified by Copernicus's theories. Luther was leader of the attack on corruption in the Roman Catholic Church that resulted in the movement called the Reformation. The movement led to the formation of the Protestant branch of Christianity. Pointing out that "sacred Scripture tells us that Joshua commanded the Sun to stand still, and not the Earth," Luther dismissed Copernicus as an astrologer and a fool.

Copernicus had already presented his theory of a Sun-centered universe to Pope Clement VII in 1533. His reluctance to publish his ideas seems to have reflected concerns about people misunderstanding his arguments rather than threats from the Church. Copernicus claimed he had deliberately made his work as technical as possible so that it could be judged only by experts. On the title page of his book, he printed a motto taken from Plato's Academy. It read, "Let no one enter who knows no Geometry."

Getting the Theory Published

Copernicus may not have published *On the Revolutions of the Celestial Spheres* but for Georg Joachim von Lauchen, an Austrian-born mathematician also known as Rheticus. He had learned of Copernicus's theory of a Sun-centered universe in Wittenberg, Germany. In 1540, Rheticus published a brief description of it in *First Account of the Book On the Revolutions by Nicolaus Copernicus*. Rheticus managed to persuade Copernicus to have his manuscript printed so that it could be circulated to a wider public.

Unknown to Copernicus, however, an addition had been made to his text before the book was printed. Rheticus showed the text to a priest named Andreas Osiander, who was a supporter of Luther. Osiander inserted a preface saying that Copernicus's theory was only a way of tying in calculations with observations, and that it should not be taken literally. This explanation may have been intended to make the work more acceptable to the public. By the time the book was finally published, Copernicus had suffered a stroke. A first copy of the printed edition is said to have been presented to him on the day he died.

Shifting Stars

Copernicus's ideas were now revealed to other astronomers, the Church, and the public. The most important astronomical criticism came from the Dane Tycho Brahe. He argued that, if Earth were orbiting the Sun once a year, then anyone observing the stars regularly would view them from widely different observational points during the course of the year, and would expect to see a shift in the star patterns. Astronomers of the time could not see a shift, so they decided that Earth could not be moving. In fact, the shift does take place. It is called annual parallax.

Copernicus had considered this point. He was convinced that parallax could not be seen only because the stars were so far away from Earth. This was another point of dispute, however, because most astronomers of the time could not imagine that God would design a universe with huge spaces between the stars and the planets. Copernicus was right, however. Annual parallax was detected in 1838 by the German astronomer Friedrich Bessel. Satellites and telescopes now provide accurate measurements of parallax angles for stars up to 10,000 **light-years** from Earth.

In 1632, Italian scientist Galileo Galilei published *Dialogue Concerning the Two Chief World Systems*, in which he supported Copernicus's view over that of Ptolemy.

EXTENSION ACTIVITY

More

Rheticus

Analyze the text about the life of Georg Joachim von Lauchen, known as Rheticus.

1. Why might Rheticus have left Austria to join Copernicus in Poland? Formulate some possible theories to explain this.
2. Are astronomy and mathematics similar? Why or why not? Why might Rheticus have been doing research in both fields? Formulate some hypotheses.

First Hand

To His Holiness, Pope Paul III

Analyze the text of Nicolaus Copernicus's preface to his book *On the Revolutions*.

1. What is Copernicus's opinion about the work of philosophers? Why did he hesitate to officially publish his theory? How does he justify this hesitation?
2. Why might Copernicus dedicate his book to the pope? Why did he think the Catholic Church would benefit from his theory? Support your answer with excerpts from the text.

RUBRIC

Analyzing a Scientific Video

Students will watch and assess a video related to a scientific discovery, and write an analysis of the video. An exemplary video analysis will meet the following criteria.

- Identifies the purpose of the video
- Identifies the intended audience of the video
- Identifies the video as a primary or secondary source
- Discusses the scientific and social context of the video
- Describes how the content of the video is presented
- Summarizes the information and opinions presented in the video
- Analyzes the quality of the content presented in the video
- Assesses the effectiveness of the video
- Determines whether the images and graphics used in the video relate to the content
- Determines whether the video is easy to follow and understand
- Gives the analysis a clear and consistent purpose
- Organizes the analysis in a logical, effective manner
- Presents a strong, clear argument about the video
- Provides strong and accurate details to support the argument about the video
- Considers other perspectives on the purpose and effectiveness of the video
- Cites all sources used in the analysis

Galileo Galilei made highly significant contributions to the fields of gravitation, motion, and astronomy. His methods made him the first truly "modern" scientist. He clashed with the Catholic Church, however, over his views about the shape of the universe.

GALILEO GALILEI

1564–1642

Galileo Galilei was born in 1564 in Pisa, in Italy. In 1581, he enrolled at the University of Pisa to study medicine, but his real interest lay in mathematics, and he began to devote all his spare time to it, becoming a lecturer in mathematics at the university in 1589. Throughout his life, Galileo was constantly short of money. In 1592, he moved to work in Padua, which had a larger university that paid him more money. While there, he met Marina Gamba, and they had three children.

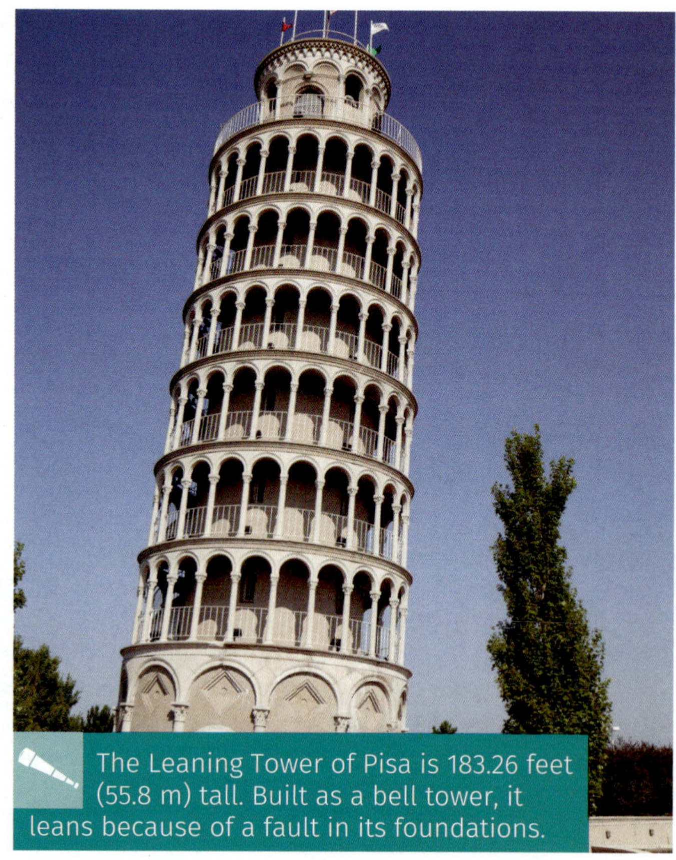

The Leaning Tower of Pisa is 183.26 feet (55.8 m) tall. Built as a bell tower, it leans because of a fault in its foundations.

Discovery through Experiment

Galileo preferred to experiment rather than to deduce facts through theory alone. He presented his results in everyday Italian and in lively, readable prose. This meant that his work reached a wider public than other scientific publications.

While at Padua, Galileo began investigating motion. He proved that a projectile such as an arrow shot from a bow does not travel in a straight line and then drop to the ground, as the ancient Greek philosopher Aristotle had believed. Galileo found that the projectile travels in a curve known as a parabola. He also wrestled with other problems of motion, such as falling objects. Aristotle's view had been that the rate at which an object falls is related to its weight, so that a large, heavy rock would fall faster than a small, light pea. If both were released from the same height, Aristotle argued that the heavier body would reach the ground first.

Galileo disagreed. He thought that all objects fall through the air at the same speed. He is said to have traveled to Pisa in 1591 to test his theory. According to the story, Galileo took two cannon balls to the top of the Leaning Tower of Pisa. One ball weighed 10 pounds (4.5 kilograms), and the other just 1 pound (0.45 kg). Galileo released the balls at precisely the same time, and both struck the ground simultaneously.

Although this story has been told of Galileo for centuries, the experiment was in fact carried out by a rival hoping to prove Galileo wrong. If he had dropped a cannon ball and a sheet of paper, air resistance would have kept the sheet of paper fluttering in the air for longer. The two cannon balls, despite their different weights, were of similar shape, so they plummeted to the ground with equal force.

Exciting Discoveries

Galileo came to accept the theory of the Polish astronomer Nicolaus Copernicus that the planets revolved around the Sun, but he was reluctant to make his views public. The theory contradicted the teachings of the Catholic Church. Things changed once Galileo heard news of a recent invention that had been made in Flanders, which is now Belgium.

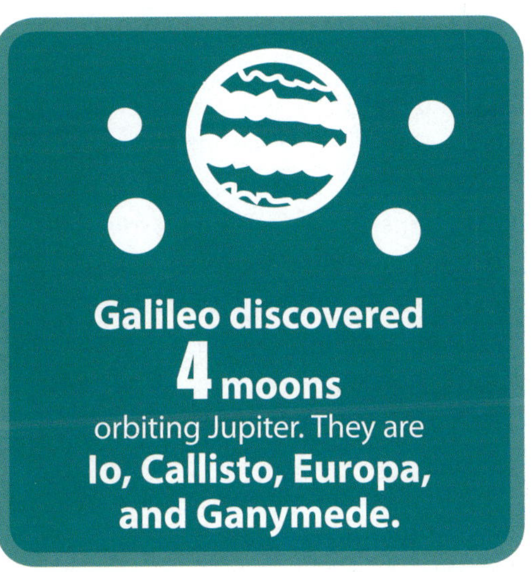

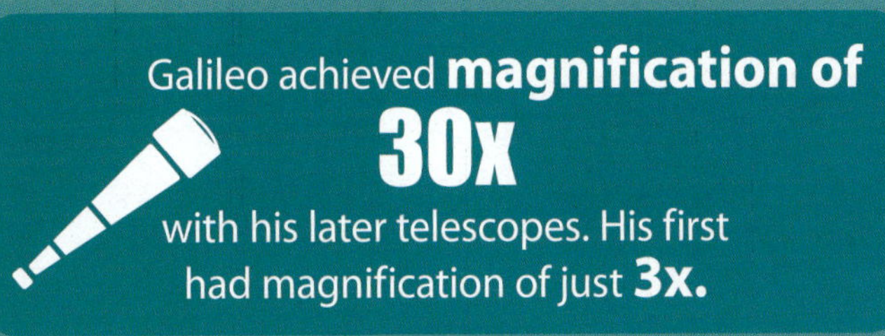

Galileo designed and built **a geometric and military compass.** He sold **100 compasses** for 20 lire, and charged 120 lire to teach people how to use them.

EXTENSION ACTIVITY

Video

Galileo's "falling bodies" experiment recreated at Pisa

Analyze the video of the "falling bodies" experiment's recreation.

1. Who recreated the experiment? In your opinion, why was the experiment recreated in this way? Why was the experiment recreated, despite the uncertainty over whether it was performed in the first place?
2. What did the "falling bodies" experiments set out to prove? Describe the experiment in your own words. How did Galileo's theory on falling bodies connect with other scientific theories?

Weblink

Copernicus' revolution and Galileo's vision: our changing view of the universe in pictures

Interpret the graphic representations of the theories of Galilei, Copernicus, and Kepler.

1. In your opinion, why are these theories also associated with specific graphic representations? Formulate some hypotheses. How are the graphic representations similar? How do they differ? Justify your answer.
2. How was the observation of the planets' movements important to the formulation of these theories? Why was Ptolemy's estimation of the position of the planets substantially correct, even if his theory was not? Formulate some hypotheses.

The telescope built by Galileo was not just useful for astronomy. At a time when most trade was conducted by ship, it also helped sailors to navigate.

"About ten months ago," Galileo wrote in around 1609, "a report reached my ears that a certain Fleming [an inhabitant of Flanders] had constructed a certain spyglass [a telescope] by means of which visible objects though very distant from the eye of the observer were distinctly seen as if nearby." Galileo set about producing a similar instrument. He prepared a hollow lead tube and fitted two glass lenses at either end. One was concave, meaning that it curved inward on one side, and the other was convex and curved outward on one side. He placed his eye to the concave lens and found that distant objects appeared three to nine times larger than seen with the naked eye. He then made a more accurate instrument that enlarged distant objects more than 60 times.

Using the Telescope

While watching the planet Jupiter with his telescope on January 7, 1610, Galileo saw something strange. He spotted three objects close to Jupiter, two on one side and one on the other. The objects, which he took to be stars, lay in a straight line. The next night, Galileo saw three objects to the west of Jupiter and none to the east. Two nights later, two objects were visible to the east and none to the west. Galileo concluded that there were three stars "wandering around Jupiter, like Venus and Mercury around the Sun." He later revised the number to four. As they circled the planet, they were sometimes lost from sight behind it or visible from Earth to its east or west. Although Galileo called them stars, they were actually Jupiter's moons, or satellites.

Galileo took his telescope to Bologna to show it to his colleagues, but the demonstration was not successful. Martin Horky, an astronomer from Bohemia in the modern Czech Republic, was a pupil of German astronomer Johannes Kepler. He claimed that the telescope worked well while observing earthly objects, but produced "fictions" when pointed at the heavens. Others proved unwilling even to look through the telescope.

Until this date, astronomers had believed that the heavenly bodies, including the Moon, were perfectly smooth and spherical. Observing the Moon through his telescope, Galileo discovered that it had mountains. Galileo was also amazed by the vast numbers of stars that his telescope revealed for the first time. He turned his attention to the galaxy, or Milky Way, which is visible as a hazy band of light in the night sky. Since ancient times, philosophers and scientists had puzzled over the precise nature of this spectacle. Galileo settled their disputes once and for all. He concluded that, "The galaxy is nothing else but a mass of innumerable stars planted together in clusters."

Anxious to ensure that his discovery of the moons of Jupiter would be properly rewarded, Galileo named them "the Medicean Stars" in honor of the Medici rulers of Tuscany. In this way, he hoped to make his reputation and earn a higher salary. He also dedicated the account of his discovery to the then-ruler of Tuscany, Grand Duke Cosimo II. The flattery paid off. In 1610, the duke made Galileo his principal mathematician, and the scientist was able to arrange his return to Florence, where the duke lived.

Challenging Long-held Views

Galileo was by now seen to be challenging the centuries-old authority of Aristotle and the Greek philosophers, and his views offended many people. In 1612, he became involved in a dispute about the properties, or characteristics, of ice. Galileo argued that ice floats on water because its density, which is its volume and **mass**, is less than that of water. His opponents, following Aristotle, said it was due to its wide, flat shape. The argument became so unpleasant that Cosimo II ruled that the debate be stopped in public.

In 1613, Galileo became involved in an argument with the German astronomer Christoph Scheiner, a Jesuit priest. Galileo was convinced that he had been the first to observe spots on the surface of the Sun in 1611. Now, two years later, he thought Scheiner was seeking to claim credit for the discovery. Furthermore, Scheiner believed that the spots could not exist on the Sun itself, as this would imply that the Sun was changeable, whereas Aristotle had said that it was perfect and unchanging. Scheiner decided that sunspots must be satellites orbiting in space between Earth and the Sun. Galileo pointed out that, when the sunspots were at the outer edge of the Sun, they seemed to move more slowly than when they were at its center. He correctly reasoned that the change in their speed would make sense if the sunspots formed part of the Sun. They would be unlikely, however, if they existed independently of the Sun.

The shadow of Earth falling on the Moon casts an uneven line, which showed Galileo that the Moon's surface is covered with jagged mountains and round craters.

EXTENSION ACTIVITY

First Hand

A Discourse Presented to the Most Serene Don Cosimo II.

Examine Galileo's letter of dedication to Cosimo II of his discourse concerning the natation of bodies upon or submersion in water.

1. Why is Galileo's work dedicated to the Greatduke of Tuscany? How is the text of the dedication organized? In Galileo's words, why did he decide to write this treatise?
2. Compare and contrast Galileo's dedication to the Greatduke Cosimo II and Copernicus's dedication to Pope Paul III. How are they similar? How do they differ? Support your answer using excerpts from the texts.

Weblink

Galileo and the Telescope

Explore how Galileo used and improved the telescope in his scientific research.

1. How did the telescope facilitate Galileo's research? How did his improvements to the telescope influence his work? Justify your answers with references.
2. What did Galileo discover using the telescope? Why might Galileo have reported his findings using drawings? How would Galileo's research have changed without the telescope? How would it have changed with a different technology? Formulate some theories and evaluate them.

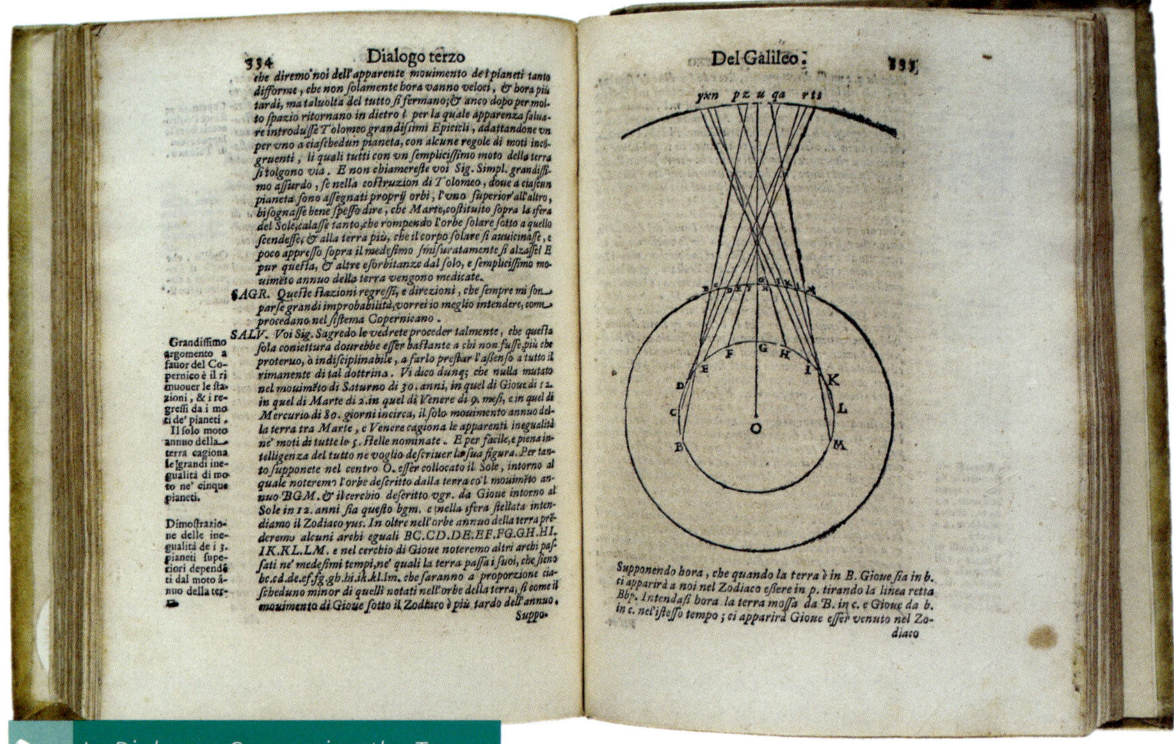

334 Dialogo terzo

che diremo noi dell'apparente mouimento de i pianeti tanto difforme, che non solamente hora vanno veloci, & hora più tardi, ma taluolta del tutto si fermano; & anco dopo per molto spazio ritornano in dietro! per la quale apparenza saluare introdusse Tolomeo grandissimi Epicicli, adattandone vn per vno a ciaschedun pianeta, con alcune regole di moti incongruenti, li quali tutti con vn semplicissimo moto della terra si tolgono via. E non chiamereste voi Sig. Simpl. grandissimo assurdo, se nella costruzion di Tolomeo, doue a ciascun pianeta sono assegnati proprij orbi, l'vno superior all'altro, bisognasse bene spesso dire, che Marte, costituito sopra la sfera del Sole, calasse tanto, che rompendo l'orbe solare sotto a quello scendesse, & alla terra più, che il corpo solare si auuicinasse, e poco appresso sopra il medesimo smisuratamente si alzasse! E pur queste, & altre esorbitanze dal solo, e semplicissimo mouimẽto annuo della terra vengono medicate.

SAGR. Queste stazioni regressi, e direzioni, che sempre mi son parse grandi improbabilità, vorrei io meglio intendere, come procedano nel sistema Copernicano.

SALV. Voi Sig. Sagredo le vedrete proceder talmente, che questa sola coniettura dourebbe esser bastante a chi non fusse, più che proteruo, ò indisciplinabile, a farlo prestar l'assenso a tutto il rimanente di tal dottrina. Vi dico dunq; che nulla mutato nel mouimẽto di Saturno di 30. anni, in quel di Gioue di 12. in quel di Marte di 2. in quel di Venere di 9. mesi, e in quel di Mercurio di 80. giorni incirca, il solo mouimento annuo della terra tra Marte, e Venere cagiona le apparenti inegualità ne' moti di tutte le 5. stelle nominate. E per facile, e piena intelligenza del tutto ne voglio descriuer la sua figura. Per tanto supponete nel centro O. esser collocato il Sole, intorno al quale noteremo l'orbe descritto dalla terra co'l mouimẽto annuo BGM. & il cerchio descritto vgr. da Gioue intorno al Sole in 12. anni sia questo bgm. e nella sfera stellata intendiamo il Zodiaco yus. In oltre nell'orbe annuo della terra prenderemo alcuni archi eguali BC.CD.DE.EF.FG.GH.HI.IK.KL.LM. e nel cerchio di Gioue noteremo altri archi passati ne' medesimi tempi, ne' quali la terra passa i suoi, che sieno bc.cd.de.ef.fg.gh.hi.ik.kl.lm. che saranno a proporzione ciascheduno minor di quelli notati nell'orbe della terra, si come il mouimento di Gioue sotto il Zodiaco è più tardo dell'annuo.

Suppo-

Grandissimo argomento a fauor del Copernico è il rimuouer le stazioni, & i regressi da i moti de' pianeti.

Il solo moto annuo della terra cagiona le grandi inegualità di moto ne' cinque pianeti.

Dimostrazione delle inegualità de i 3. pianeti superiori dependẽti dal moto ãnuo della terra.

Del Galileo. 335

Supponendo hora, che quando la terra è in B. Gioue sia in b. ci apparirà a noi nel Zodiaco essere in p. tirando la linea retta Bbp. Intendasi hora la terra mossa da B. in c. e Gioue da b. in c. nel'istesso tempo; ci apparirà Gioue esser venuto nel Zodiaco

In *Dialogue Concerning the Two Chief World Systems*, Galileo used mathematics and diagrams to explain the orbits of the planets around Earth.

Convicted for his Views

Galileo was gathering enemies in Rome because of his views. Many of his theories challenged traditional Church doctrines, and in 1633, he stood trial before the Inquisition and received a life sentence. He was held under house arrest at Arcetri, outside Florence, where he completed his scientific masterpiece, *Discourses upon Two New Sciences* (1638), in which he brought together previously unpublished experiments that had been interrupted by his telescope studies.

He now returned to his investigations into falling objects. He had established that, when dropped from the same height, objects fall equal distances in equal times, whatever their weight. If the weight of an object does not affect the rate at which it falls, however, what does? Galileo needed to find a means of measuring accurately the rate at which objects fall. He devised several systems of his own for measuring minute intervals of time.

To aid his research, Galileo set out to find a way of slowing down as far as possible the rate at which objects fall. He rolled a smooth ball down a polished grooved slope, noting the time it took to reach the bottom. When he had repeated the experiment several times, he next rolled the ball a quarter of the length of the groove. His measurements showed that the ball took half the time to travel this distance as it took to travel the full length of the groove. By repeating these experiments many times for different lengths of the grove, Galileo showed that the distance covered by a falling object was proportional to the square of the time taken. If an object falls 6 feet (1.83 m) in one second, for example, then in two seconds it will fall 2^2 (four times) as far.

In three seconds, it will fall 3^2 (nine times) as far, so it will fall 9 x 6 feet, or 54 feet (16.47 m), and so on. Galileo had found that, as an object falls, it accelerates at a uniform rate. He had proved by experiments what the great scientist Isaac Newton would later describe in his second law of motion.

Galileo remained under house arrest at Arcetri until his death. He was allowed visitors, however. Galileo was also permitted to continue with his research and to write. He began a new book on the sciences of motion and strength of materials. The last discoveries made with his telescope, in 1637, noted how the Moon appeared to wobble in its orbit both daily and monthly. By this time, Galileo was suffering from high blood pressure, arthritis, and failing eyesight. He died at Arcetri in January 1642. Since his death, his scientific reputation has grown.

Galileo realized that a pendulum swings at a set rate after seeing a swinging lamp in Pisa Cathedral. The insight helped lead to the creation of the pendulum clock.

A BELATED PARDON

Even after Galileo's death, the Church authorities continued their feud with him. The scientist was not permitted a public funeral, or allowed to be buried next to his father and other family members. Although a number of memorials to Galileo can be seen today in Florence, they were all built long after his death. In 1559, the papal authorities introduced an Index of Prohibited Books. This consisted of a list of books that the Church considered unsuitable to be read by ordinary men and women because of the views they expressed. Any reader of one of these books faced possible excommunication, or exclusion from the Church. The works of Copernicus were placed on the index in 1616, and in 1664, Galileo's *Dialogue Concerning the Two Chief World Systems* was also added. Galileo's work was not removed from the list until 1835, and it was only in 1992, 350 years after Galileo's death, that Pope John Paul II formally announced that the Inquisition had been wrong to condemn Galileo. The pope finally admitted that Galileo had been right to claim that the Bible could not always be taken literally.

EXTENSION ACTIVITY

More

Galileo's Contribution to Science
Explore why Galileo's work is still considered important.

1. In your opinion, why was Galileo's importance not recognized during his lifetime? How might he have been regarded, had he lived and worked today?
2. What did Galileo mean when he described the world as a book of nature? Justify your answer.

Document

The Crime of Galileo: Indictment, Sentence, and Abjuration of 1633
Analyze the text of Galileo's indictment, sentence, and abjuration.

1. According to the indictment, what was Galileo accused of? Who was accusing him? Why were Galileo's theories considered "heresy"?
2. How do you explain the content of the abjuration? In your opinion, who wrote this text?
3. Why did Galileo have to officially reject his theory? What might have happened had he refused to comply?

ANTOINE LAVOISIER

1743–1794

Among Antoine Lavoisier's achievements are his explanation of the chemical basis of combustion, or burning, and his modern redefinition of the elements. His career was interrupted by the events of the French Revolution. He was eventually executed by the revolutionary forces.

Antoine Laurent Lavoisier was born in Paris on August 26, 1743. He was educated in law, but his real interests lay in **chemistry**, astronomy, and mathematics. After Lavoisier graduated in law in 1763, he wrote a paper on the mineral gypsum, which he presented at the Academy of Sciences. Lavoisier needed an income, so in 1768, the year he was elected to the Academy, he bought a stake in the General Farm. This was an agency used by the government to collect taxes. The decision would have dramatic consequences.

New Discoveries

Lavoisier began to work for the Academy of Science. He prepared reports on subjects ranging from early balloon flight to the manufacture of gunpowder. In 1768, the Academy wanted to find out whether water supplied to Paris through a canal was fit to drink.

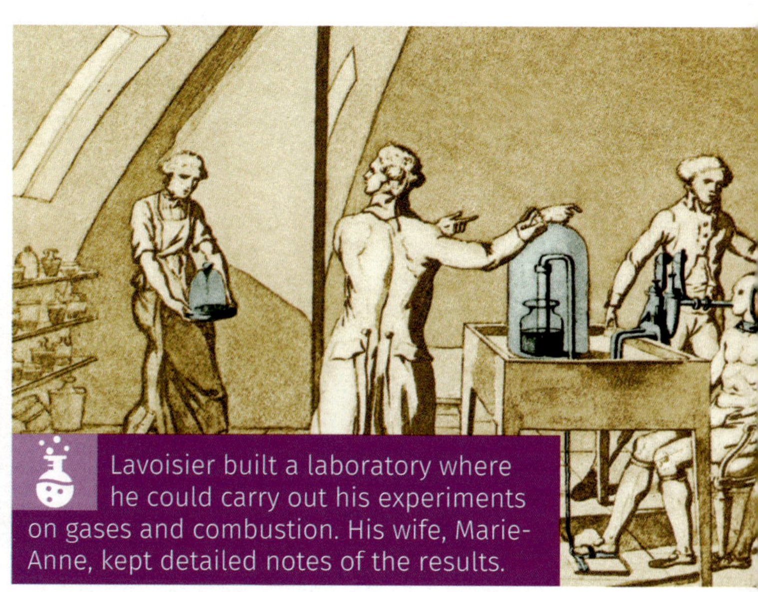

Lavoisier built a laboratory where he could carry out his experiments on gases and combustion. His wife, Marie-Anne, kept detailed notes of the results.

The usual way to test for impurities was to boil water dry to see what solids were left. This led Lavoisier to wonder if one substance, such as water, could be changed into another, such as earth. Medieval **alchemists** believed that substances could be changed into others when heated. Even in the late eighteenth century, some scientists argued that water turned into earth on heating. They based this conclusion on the fact that, when pure rainwater was distilled in a glass vessel, it left behind solid **matter**, or "earth." Lavoisier showed that this "earth" was dissolved, or leached, from the glass itself during the boiling process.

Lavoisier then investigated what takes place when things are burned, a process called combustion. According to German chemist Georg Stahl, all substances were made up of water and three varieties of earth, one of which was combustible. This was set free into the air when the substance was burned. He called it phlogiston, from the Greek word for "burned." According to Stahl, metals burned because they lost phlogiston into the air. In fact, scientists now know that metals burn by uniting with oxygen in the air.

The English chemist Joseph Priestley carried out experiments into the nature of combustion in England at the same time Lavoisier was working in France.

In 1771, Louis-Bernard Guyton de Morveau showed that metals grew heavier when burned in air. However, if phlogiston was lost during combustion, metals would lose weight. Guyton concluded that metals became heavier when "dephlogisticated," because phlogiston was weightless and buoyed up the materials containing it. Lavoisier thought it more likely that "air," which was then the term used for a gas, was involved in combustion, and that this air caused the increase in weight.

Understanding Combustion

Lavoisier burned many substances and measured how their weight changed. He concluded that phosphorus and sulfur got heavier when burned because they absorbed air. He then reversed the process by burning a burned metallic residue, or calx, with charcoal. Scientists now know calx is an oxide, formed when a substance mixes with oxygen. After burning, the metal weighed less than the original calx, suggesting that it had lost the air absorbed in the original burning.

EXTENSION ACTIVITY

More

Joseph Priestley

Assess the importance of Joseph Priestley's scientific contributions.

1. Why did Priestley refuse to abandon the phlogiston theory, despite his own discoveries about oxygen? Formulate some hypotheses.
2. How could Priestley's previous interest in electricity have led to his research in chemistry? How is electricity linked to chemistry? Research possible reasons to justify your answer.

Weblink

Antoine Lavoisier: Father of Modern Chemistry

Explore the scientific achievements of Antoine Lavoisier by reading the text and watching the associated videos.

1. What made Lavoisier a wealthy man? In your opinion, did his wealth influence his scientific research? Why or why not? Justify your answer.
2. How was Lavoisier's research influenced by Priestley's discoveries? In what ways were Priestley's and Lavoisier's work similar? How were they different? Support your answer with examples from the text.
3. Why might Marie-Anne Lavoisier be described as the mother of modern chemistry? Suppose she was alive today. How might her observations be regarded?

RUBRIC

Create a Scientific Drawing

Create a scientific drawing illustrating an object or design. An exemplary scientific drawing will meet the following criteria.

- Includes a descriptive and accurate title
- The drawing(s) realistically depicts the object(s)
- The drawing only includes features that were actually observed
- Relevant details such as size, colors, textures, shapes, and relationships to surroundings are included
- Multiple perspectives are drawn to provide the viewer with a complete picture
- All parts of the scientific drawing are clearly labeled with the correct terms
- A written explanation of the drawing shows what is included in the drawing
- A key or legend is provided
- An appropriate size and scale is chosen for the drawing so that the details are easily recognized

Lavoisier learned that British chemists had discovered that the **atmosphere** is made up of different "airs." In the 1750s, Scottish chemist Joseph Black found that some substances contained an air, now known as carbon dioxide, that was heavier than normal air and did not burn. Then, English chemist Henry Cavendish found that a light, inflammable air was produced when a mix of water and sulfuric acid was poured over iron.

In 1774, the English chemist Joseph Priestley heated oxide of mercury in a closed vessel and collected a gas in which things burned better than in ordinary air. Lavoisier carried out some experiments to reveal that this "purest part of air" was the active agent of burning. The new part of air Priestley had discovered burned carbon to form the weak acid carbon dioxide, and Lavoisier named it "oxygen," meaning "acid-former." He now correctly asserted that combustion occurs when oxygen combines with another substance, releasing heat and light, and causing that substance to increase in weight.

It remained difficult to explain why an inflammable gas was produced when dilute acid was poured on metal. Lavoisier found the answer through Cavendish's discovery that, when oxygen and the inflammable gas were exploded by a spark, moisture covered the sides of the vessel. Cavendish concluded that this was water. To Lavoisier, the experiment showed that water is made up of oxygen and the inflammable gas. Lavoisier gave this gas the name "hydrogen," or "water-forming." He could now explain why hydrogen was given off when metal was dissolved in dilute acid. It came not from the metal but from the water in the dilute acid as it was broken down into its parts of oxygen and hydrogen.

Lavoisier used a lens called a burning glass to focus the Sun's rays in order to ignite chemicals. In 1784, he built a large version for the Academy of Sciences.

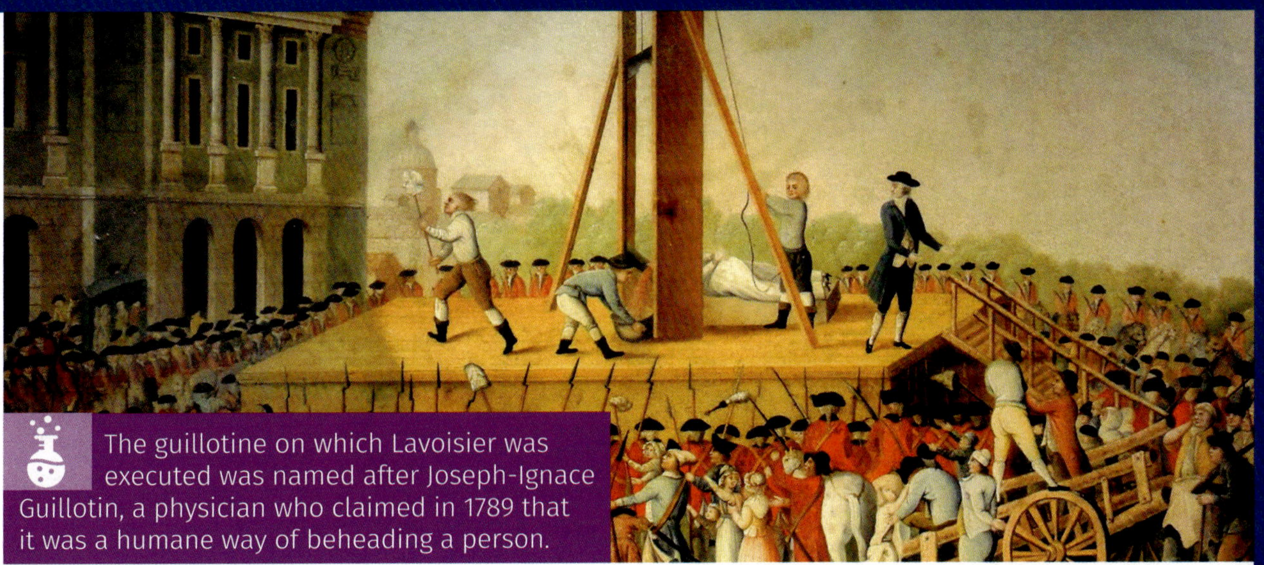

The guillotine on which Lavoisier was executed was named after Joseph-Ignace Guillotin, a physician who claimed in 1789 that it was a humane way of beheading a person.

The New Chemistry

Lavoisier now redefined elements as any substance that cannot be broken down. Hydrogen and oxygen are elements. Water, however, is a **compound** made up of hydrogen and oxygen. Lavoisier and his followers founded a journal in 1788 in which they shared their ideas, *Annals of Chemistry*, which still exists. In 1789, Lavoisier published *An Elementary Treatise of Chemistry*. Written in clear language, it became the chemistry textbook for many decades.

Lavoisier also carried out experiments to show that animal respiration, or breathing, is a form of combustion. The oxygen that a living being breathes in burns the carbon in foodstuffs. This chemical reaction releases heat and also produces carbon dioxide, which is breathed out. This work laid the foundations of biochemistry. In July 1789, however, the French Revolution broke out. Lavoisier's association with the old government made him a target of the revolutionaries. He was executed by guillotine in May 1794.

Marie-Anne Lavoisier

Although Marie-Anne Pierrette Paulze, whom Lavoisier married in 1771, was not a trained scientist herself, she made an important contribution to science through the work she shared with her husband. She assisted him in his laboratory and, having studied art specially for the purpose, prepared the illustrations in his *Treatise of Chemistry*. She also learned English so that she would be able to translate the scientific works of Henry Cavendish and Joseph Priestley for her husband to study. Her final service for Lavoisier was to collect and edit his *Memoirs of Chemistry* (1803), after his death. In 1805, Marie-Anne married the American-born scientist Sir Benjamin Thompson, Count Rumford, who was particularly known for his work on heat. However, the couple separated in 1809.

EXTENSION ACTIVITY

More

A Date with the Guillotine
Evaluate the effects of the French Revolution on Lavoisier's scientific research.

1. Why were Lavoisier's letters about scientific research grounds for a death sentence? Discuss some possible reasons.
2. Why was Lavoisier not allowed to finish his research before his sentence was carried out? What does "the Republic has no need of experts" mean?
3. What do you think of the French revolutionary authorities' actions against Lavoisier? Justify your answer.

Weblink

Revolutionary Instruments: Lavoisier's Tools as Objets d'Art
Analyze the function of Lavoisier's chemical equipment in a famous portrait and in Lavoisier's *Elements of Chemistry*.

1. Why might these specific pieces of equipment have been represented in Jacques Louis David's portrait of Lavoisier and his wife? Justify your answer.
2. Why did Lavoisier describe in detail his equipment using illustrations in his *Elements of Chemistry*? Do the drawings of equipment in Lavoisier's book have the same purpose as in David's portrait? Why or why not?

ALEXANDER VON HUMBOLDT

1769–1859

In an age when scientists turned to careful observation, measurement, and experiment in order to reassess and understand the natural world, the Prussian nobleman Alexander von Humboldt founded a range of new scientific disciplines.

Friedrich Wilhelm Heinrich Alexander von Humboldt was born in Berlin on September 14, 1769. When he enrolled at the University of Göttingen as a student, Humboldt became interested in natural science. While there, he met the German naturalist Georg Forster, who had previously sailed with the English navigator Captain James Cook on his voyages to the Pacific Ocean. Forster's experiences may have inspired Humboldt to later journey to South America.

In 1791, Humboldt graduated from the Freiberg School of Mining. Based on the study of rocks and fossils, many scientists of the time were beginning to conclude that Earth was far more than a few thousand years old, which was the theory according to the Biblical account of creation. What Humboldt saw on his later travels led him to accept the theory of Scottish geologist James Hutton, who said that Earth was formed over millions of years, and that it was still going through a process of change and development.

Traveling to South America

When his mother died in 1796, Humboldt inherited a share of the family fortune. This money allowed him to indulge his passion for travel. He and the French botanist Aimé Bonpland decided to visit South America, which had rivers, grasslands, rainforests, mountains, and high plateaus.

Humboldt and Bonpland lived and worked in temporary camps in the rainforest as they explored the Orinoco and Amazon rivers.

It had been 50 years since the last scientific expedition to the region. Humboldt and Bonpland hoped to research and explore the **geography**, wildlife, and plants of the continent. They set sail in 1799, and eventually landed in Caracas, Venezuela.

In February 1800, the two men headed inland. The first part of their expedition was a journey of 1,725 miles (2,775 kilometers) through wild, unexplored country. They encountered many new animals and plants, and established that the Orinoco and Amazon River systems are linked. They then traveled through the mountains of the Andes. Near Quito, they prepared to climb Mount Chimborazo, a 20,569-foot (6,269-m) volcano in Ecuador. In June 1802, they climbed Chimborazo to about 18,893 feet (5,762 m), setting a world altitude record at the time.

30 years
The time Humboldt and Bonpland held **the world altitude record** for mountain climbing

11 The number of plant and animal species named in honor of Humboldt—**more than any other person**

6,000 miles (9,650 km)
The distance Humboldt and Bonpland **traveled during their 5 years** in the Americas

EXTENSION ACTIVITY

Video

Alexander von Humboldt - The Great Explorer
Examine Alexander von Humboldt's contributions to natural science.

1. Did wealth influence Alexander von Humboldt's work? Why or why not? What motivated Humboldt to leave the civil service and embark on his travels? Formulate some hypotheses.
2. How did Humboldt feel nature should be observed? Why was he interested in such a range of disciplines? How does this attitude differ from the approach of modern scientists?

Weblink

Alexander von Humboldt's *Personal Narrative of Travels to the Equinoctial Regions of America*
Assess the importance of Humboldt's book, *Personal Narrative of Travels to the Equinoctial Regions of America.*

1. In your opinion, why was Humboldt's account of his travels so stimulating for other scientists, such as Charles Darwin and John Muir? Formulate some hypotheses.
2. What information and stories does Humboldt include in his book? Why have Humboldt's observations made him "the father of biogeology"? Justify your answer.

Humboldt and Bonpland recorded and drew many plants and animals new to European science, including a black-headed uakari they kept as a pet.

Discoveries in Earth Sciences

Humboldt was a pioneer in the field now known as **earth sciences**. He aimed to show how everything was linked, so that he could understand "nature as a whole." By studying the volcanoes in Ecuador, Humboldt found that they lie above faults, or fractures, deep in Earth's crust. He also observed that many of the rocks on Earth's surface are of igneous origin. "Igneous" means fiery, and the presence of the rocks showed that they were clearly formed in conditions of extreme heat.

Humboldt was also fascinated by Earth's **magnetic field**. He mapped Earth's magnetism over a substantial area on his travels, and concluded that it was strongest at the North and South Poles and weakest at the equator. He also noted a phenomenon that he called "magnetic storms" when the magnetic field became disturbed. In the twentieth century, scientists discovered that these disturbances are caused by solar winds, which are electrically charged material thrown out by the Sun. Humboldt's other major project was the collection of data on meteorology, which is the science of the weather.

Back in Europe

When Humboldt returned to Europe from South America, he was asked to help negotiate a peace settlement in the war between France and Prussia. In 1808, he moved to Paris. He lived there for most of the next 21 years, writing up accounts of his journeys and discoveries. By the time Humboldt had finished writing his account of his travels, his fortune was almost gone. When Frederick William III of Prussia offered him a post managing the king's household, Humboldt accepted. In 1827, he returned to Berlin, where he stayed for the rest of his life. Humboldt's travels were not over, however. In 1829, he was invited by Tsar Nicholas I of Russia to travel to the gold and platinum mines of in the Ural Mountains, and to visit Central Asia. On the journey, Humboldt made many valuable observations about **geology**, geography, and meteorology.

Back in Berlin, Humboldt divided his time between research, writing, and his duties at court. He also spoke out against slavery, which he had seen in Cuba. He inspired the nationalist Simón Bolívar to liberate Venezuela and other Latin American countries from colonial rule.

For the last 20 years or so of his life, Humboldt was engaged in writing his ambitious work *Cosmos*. His aim was to present a description of Earth in which all the sciences were drawn together. He also hoped to counter what he saw as the romantic, anti-scientific philosophies that were becoming popular at the time. The book was the first comprehensive encyclopedia of geography and geology. *Cosmos* appeared in five volumes between 1845 and 1862. When Humboldt died on May 6, 1859, he was given a state funeral by the Prussian king.

To travel along rivers, the explorers used large rafts with sails and living quarters on board, which were commonly used in Peru.

A NEW APPROACH

When Alexander von Humboldt and Aimé Bonpland climbed Mount Chimborazo in Ecuador in 1802, they set an altitude record for a mountain ascent. Humboldt also took careful notes of what kind of vegetation and animals occurred at different elevations above sea level. These ranged from mushrooms at the base of the mountain through forests to the lichens at the top, near the snow line. After the climb, he recorded the information on a diagram (below). This was one of the first diagrams anyone had created to show the distribution of animals in **ecological** zones. Humboldt became a pioneer of what is now known as biogeography, or the impact of geographical features, such as mountains and coasts, and factors, such as average temperature and rainfall, on the natural biography of a region. He argued that it was impossible to study plants and animals in isolation, which was the usual approach at the time. Instead, he argued that biologists had to consider the natural world as a series of interlocking networks that exist on a regional, national, or even global level, an approach he referred to as looking at "nature as whole."

EXTENSION ACTIVITY

First Hand

Reflections on the Different Degrees of Enjoyment Presented to Us by the Aspect of Nature and the Study of Her Laws.

Analyze the introduction to Alexander von Humboldt's *Cosmos*.

1. What is the tone of this text? To what public is it addressed?
2. What are the main characteristics of nature? How is nature governed? How should a scientist approach the study of nature, according to Humboldt? Support your answers using excerpts from the text.
3. What is the "sense of enjoyment"? How did Alexander von Humboldt experience it? Have you ever experienced a similar feeling? How would you compare your experience with that of Humboldt?

Weblink

Alexander von Humboldt Digital Library | Visualization of Travels in Google Maps

Retrace the route of Alexander von Humboldt's travels in South America.

1. Which areas did Alexander von Humboldt explore? Why were Humboldt's travels concentrated in those areas? Why did he explore those specific locations? Formulate some hypotheses.
2. How do modern maps and those of Humboldt's differ? How are they similar? Defend your answer and support it using the maps.
3. How might the maps that were available to Humboldt have influenced the course of his travels? How might they influence modern-day exploration?

DMITRI MENDELEEV

1834–1907

Dmitri Mendeleev had a difficult childhood. His father went blind, then died in 1847. The family glass factory burned down, and the Mendeleevs moved from Siberia to Moscow. At school, Dmitri Mendeleev showed talent in math, **physics**, and geography. He studied at the Pedagogical Institute in St. Petersburg, qualified as a teacher in 1855, and was posted to Odessa, on the Black Sea coast in southern Russia. He obtained a degree in chemistry and traveled to Europe to continue his studies.

A founder of modern chemistry, Dmitri Mendeleev was professor of chemistry at the University of St. Petersburg. He formulated the periodic table of elements. He even predicted the existence of elements that have since been discovered. Element no. 101 is named Mendelevium for him.

	W.t		W.t
Hydrogen	1	Strontian	46
Azote	5	Barytes	68
Carbon	5.4	Iron	50
Oxygen	7	Zinc	56
Phosphorus	9	Copper	56
Sulphur	13	Lead	90
Magnesia	20	Silver	190
Lime	24	Gold	190
		ina	190
		ury	167

John Dalton calculated the atomic weight of 20 substances in 1808. However, some of the substances, such as lime, are not elements.

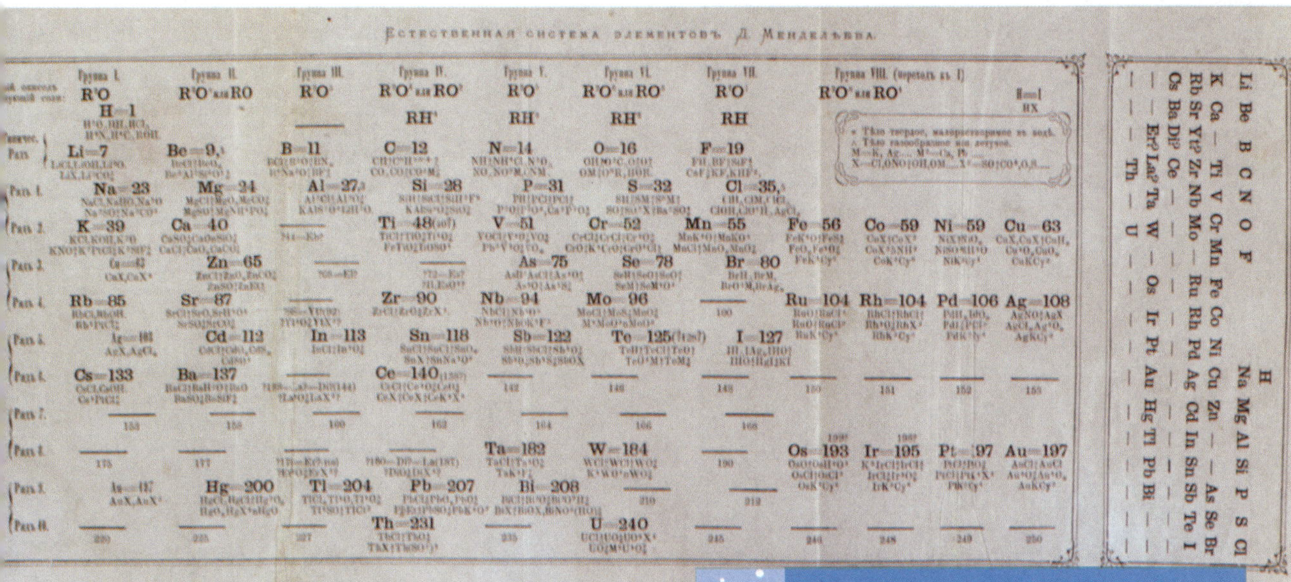

Mendeleev's first periodic table was compiled for inclusion in a student textbook he was writing. It left gaps for elements that had not yet been discovered.

Mendeleev was made professor of chemistry at the University of St. Petersburg in 1866. He devoted himself almost entirely to the study of the elements. Elements cannot be broken down into anything simpler by chemical means. All other substances are formed from them. Since the French chemist Antoine Lavoisier first defined elements, chemists had identified and named many elements. At first, they were listed in order of their date of discovery. As more were found, they were grouped according to whether they were gases or solids, metals or nonmetals. However, no one understood the relationship between the elements, or why they behave as they do.

Study of Atoms

A major contribution to understanding the elements was made by John Dalton, who studied atmospheric gases such as hydrogen and nitrogen. Some gases dissolve more readily than others in water. These, Dalton suggested, were denser, or heavier, gases. To explain how gases have different weights, Dalton developed the theory of the ancient Greek Democritus that matter consists of atoms. Dalton proposed that an atom is the smallest part of any element and cannot be created or destroyed. The atoms of a particular element are all identical, and differ from those of other elements, especially in weight.

Other scientists looked for connections between the atomic weights and properties of substances. Chlorine, bromine, and iodine, for example, act similarly in chemical reactions. German chemist Johann Döbereiner found that chlorine has an atomic weight of 35 and iodine of 127, giving an average of 81. The atomic weight of bromine is just under 80. Döbereiner found two other similarly related groups of three elements. Other chemists noted that elements with similar properties had similar weights. Iron (56), cobalt (59), and nickel (58) are all hard, magnetic metals, for example. It seemed possible to arrange the elements systematically.

EXTENSION ACTIVITY

More

John Dalton

Find out more about the life of John Dalton.

1. Describe the atomic theory and John Dalton's role in its formulation using your own words.
2. What is the difference between a mixture and a compound? Why was this difference not known until Dalton's law of partial pressures was elaborated? Formulate some hypotheses.

Video

The Periodic Table: Crash Course Chemistry #4

Review Dmitri Mendeleev's work on the periodical table.

1. In your opinion, how did Dmitri Mendeleev's family history and background influence his scientific education and accomplishments? Formulate some hypotheses.
2. How is the periodic table organized? What set Mendeleev's periodic table apart from similar systems used by other scientists working to organize chemical elements? Provide evidence to defend your ideas.

Russian rulers, such as Empress Elizabeth, supported scientists in hopes of modernizing Russia and making it a more important part of Europe.

Mendeleev's Periodic Table

Mendeleev devised a new way of classifying elements. He wrote them down in increasing order of their atomic weight, starting with lithium, a reactive metal. He saw that the seventh and the fourteenth elements after lithium, sodium and potassium, are also reactive metals. When the elements were arranged in seven columns, Mendeleev saw that the first two elements in the last column, fluorine and chlorine, are reactive nonmetals. The vertical columns on the table are "groups," and the horizontals are "periods." The elements arranged according to their atomic weight "show a periodic change of properties." Mendeleev's table came to be known as the periodic table.

Mendeleev's first periodic table contained some gaps, which he correctly predicted represented elements that had not been discovered. He went on to establish many other properties of elements in his Periodic Law, but he was unaware of one whole group on the periodic table, the "rare," or noble gases. They are very nonreactive and do not combine with other elements. The first, argon, was discovered in 1894 by the Scottish chemist William Ramsay. He went on to find three other gases present in air in small amounts, neon, krypton, and xenon. Helium was isolated by Ramsay in 1895. In 1900, the German chemist Friedrich Dorn discovered radon. The discovery of the rare gases confirmed Mendeleev's Periodic Law. They were gases, they were nonreactive, and they could be displayed in one column without conflicting with other parts of the table.

Mendeleev had other scientific interests, such as chemical fertilizers and the petroleum industry, but he was often in trouble for his progressive political views and he clashed with Russia's tsarist regime. He was removed from office in 1890, but was greatly admired and honored by the worldwide scientific community until his death in 1907. Today, he is acknowledged for providing a framework for modern chemical theory.

Atomic Numbers and New Elements

Scientists now know that an element's **atomic number** determines its chemical properties. Inside every atom is a constant number of negatively charged particles called electrons. Every atom has a central **nucleus** containing positively charged particles, or protons. The negative charges on the electrons balance the positive charges on the protons, so the atom carries no overall charge.

The atomic number of an element describes the number of protons in the nucleus of an atom. Hydrogen is the simplest atom, with just one proton in its nucleus, which is circled by a single electron. The next atom, helium, has 2 protons, iron has 26, and so on.

The more protons and electrons atoms have, the greater the weight of the atom. It does not matter if the elements are listed by their atomic weight or their atomic number. The order remains the same in the periodic table.

In 1913, Danish physicist Niels Bohr showed that electrons in an atom orbit at varying distances from the nucleus in concentric shells. This explained why elements behave in certain ways. For example, the rare gases do not react with other elements because the outermost shells of their atoms are full. They have no spare electrons for other elements and no empty spaces to accept another's electrons. In contrast, alkali metals, such as lithium and sodium, are highly reactive because they have just one electron in their outermost shell and will react with almost any other element to fill it. They are so reactive that they always occur in nature combined with another element.

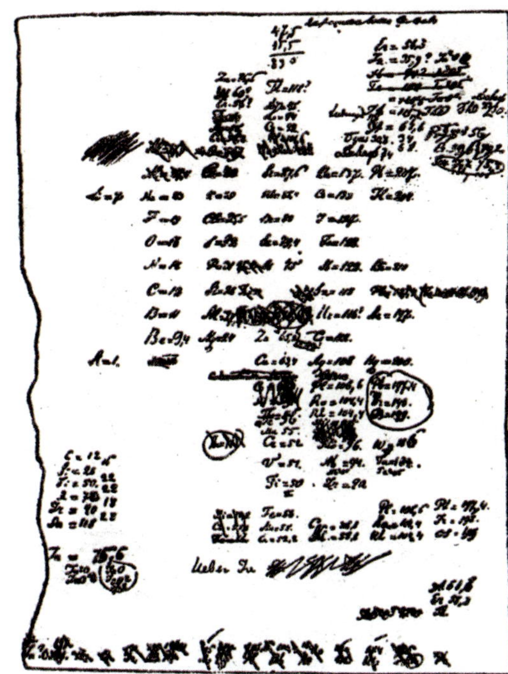

Mendeleev first began to sketch versions of the periodic table in 1869, when he listed the elements in order of their atomic weight.

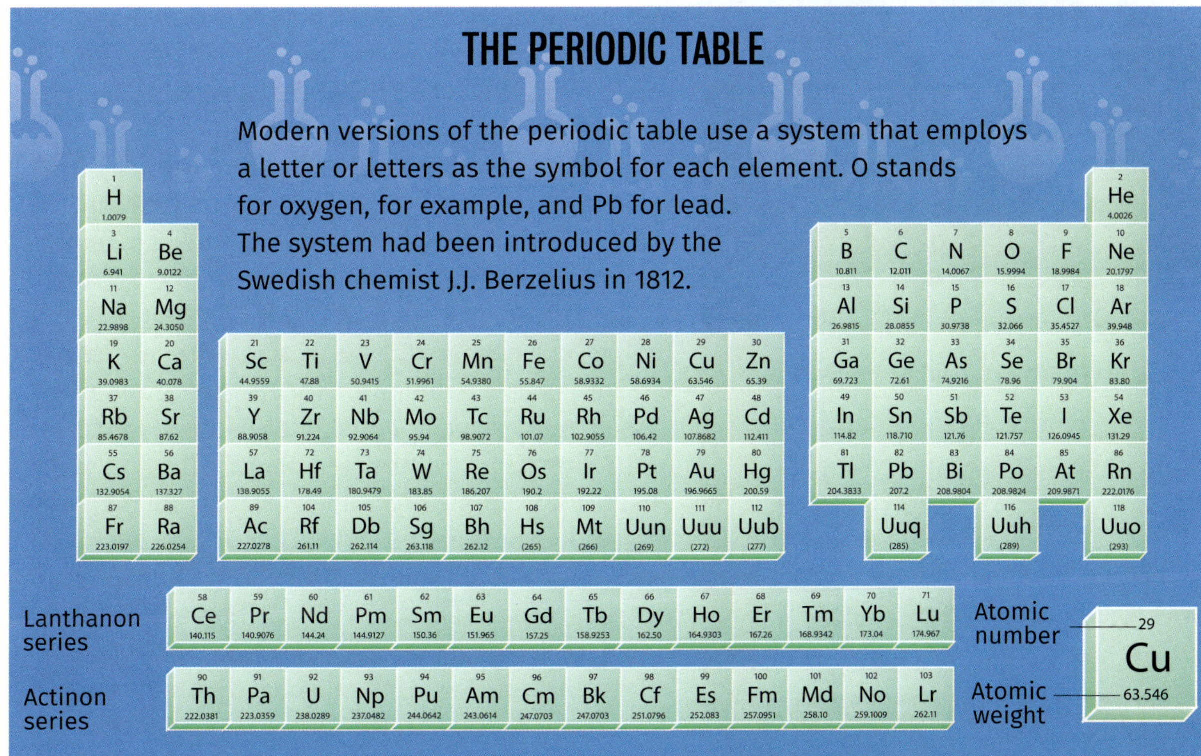

EXTENSION ACTIVITY

More

Science in Russia

Review the situation of Russian scientific research and its evolution between the nineteenth and twentieth centuries.

1. Why, in a vast territory such as Russia, were there only six universities at the beginning of the nineteenth century? Discuss some possible reasons.
2. How did the changing political situation influence the evolution of scientific research in Russia? Support your answer with examples.

Weblink

Bohr's model of the atom explains science in everyday life

Assess the importance of Niels Bohr's 1913 model of the atom.

1. Why was Bohr's model a ground-breaking discovery in 1913? How did the model of the atom evolve after that date? Support your answer by researching online for more information.
2. In which ways is Bohr's 1913 discovery linked to modern scientific research? How is it linked to daily life? Defend your answer using examples.

RUBRIC

Write an Abstract

Students will use their library or *Google Scholar* to find a scientific research article or study related to Moon formation, then write a 300-word abstract. An exemplary abstract will meet the following criteria.

- States the research question or problem that the author is answering
- Indicates the significance of the issue
- Describes and explains methods used by the scientist(s)
- Explains why the methods used by the scientist(s) were appropriate
- Explains why this article or study stands out and how it is different from others
- Clearly states how the article or study advances knowledge about the topic, why it is important, and how it can be used
- Introductory statement is clear, concise, and engaging
- Purpose is clear, concise, and relevant
- Explanation of the findings includes what was expected, discovered, accomplished, collected, and produced
- Clearly states the conclusion
- Conclusion describes how the work contributes to the field
- Writing is appropriate and free from grammatical errors

The shapes of the coastlines of Africa and South America convinced Alfred Wegener that these continents were once joined together but then drifted apart. This theory was rejected during Wegener's lifetime. It was finally accepted by scientists 30 years after his death.

ALFRED WEGENER

1880–1930

Alfred Lothar Wegener was born in Berlin, Germany, on November 1, 1880. He studied at the universities of Heidelberg, Innsbruck, and Berlin, obtaining a doctorate in astronomy in 1905. He began as an astronomer but abandoned this in favor of meteorology. In 1906, he joined a Danish expedition to Greenland as the official meteorologist. Returning to Germany, Wegener taught meteorology at the University of Marburg. In 1911, he published a book entitled *Thermodynamics of the Atmosphere*.

Continental Jigsaw Puzzles

In 1910, Wegener began to ponder the problem that occupied him for the rest of his life. From maps, it appeared that the western coastline of Africa and the eastern coastline of South America could fit together like a jigsaw puzzle. This had been noted in the sixteenth and seventeenth centuries, when the first world atlases were published. Wegener became convinced that the continents were joined together in the past, but he was not the first to suggest this.

Biologists were already aware of the similarities between fossils found in Africa and South America. Closely related species of plants and animals can occur naturally in continents thousands of miles apart. For example, marsupials, which are mammals such as kangaroos whose young are nurtured in an external pouch, live in Australia, New Guinea, and the Americas, but not in Africa or Eurasia. Southern beech trees are native only to Indonesia, Chile, Australia, and New Zealand. Such distributions are hard to explain, unless the continents had once been joined together.

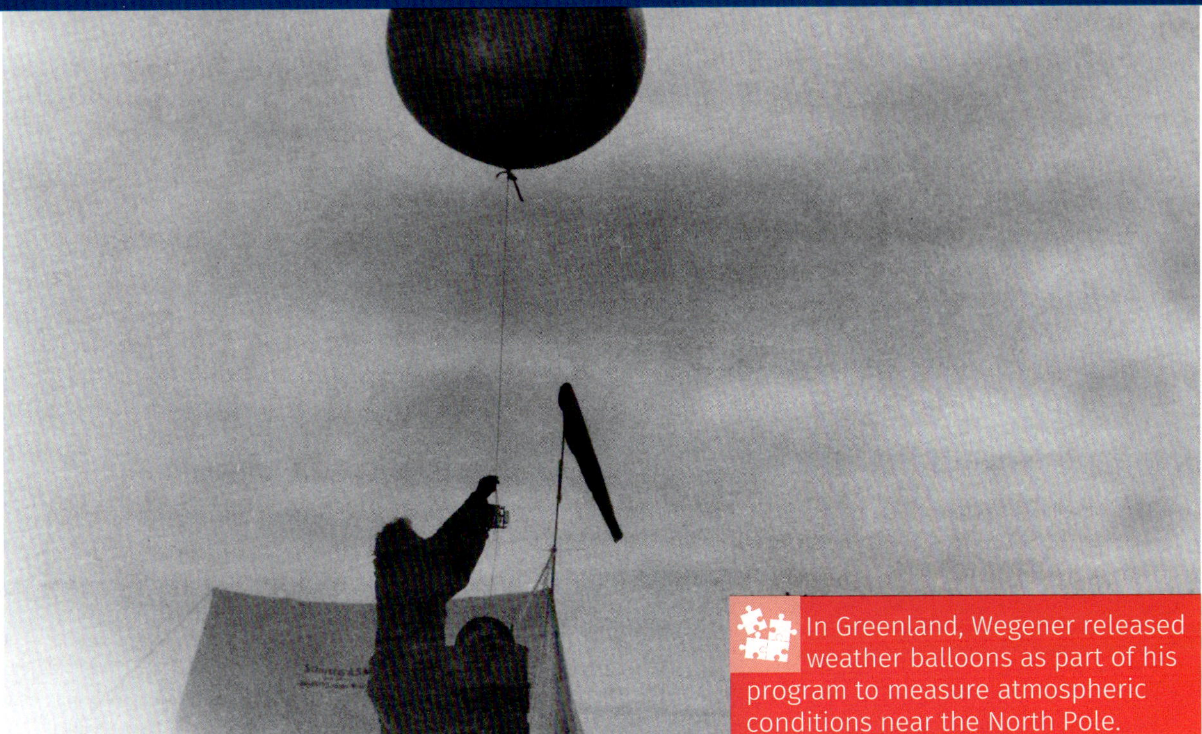

In Greenland, Wegener released weather balloons as part of his program to measure atmospheric conditions near the North Pole.

Scientists are still not sure how the Moon was formed. At the end of the nineteenth century, many believed that it had been part of Earth and had split away at some point. In 1881, English geologist Osmond Fisher suggested that the Pacific basin was the hole that the Moon had left behind. He extended this idea, claiming that, at the time of the Moon's separation, the continents had broken apart and then readjusted to Earth's new shape.

Fisher thought Earth's crust was made up of a thin layer on top of a liquid interior, and that mountains were forced upward by convection currents produced when material inside Earth heats up and drifts upward. He also thought the continents on either side of the Pacific Ocean had moved toward each other. This had caused America to split away from Eurasia and Africa, and the Atlantic had formed between them. Fisher's idea was rejected because scientists believed the interior of Earth was solid. The inner core is solid, but the outer core is semi-molten or liquid.

Pangaea and Panthalassa

Wegener was now a leading authority on Greenland. Measurements he made of the island's position suggested that, over the course of a century, Greenland had moved away from Europe by about 1 mile (1.6 km). Other measurements indicated that Washington, D.C., and Paris, France, were moving apart by about 15 feet (4.6 m) a year, and that San Diego, California, and Shanghai, China, were moving toward each other. This suggested to Wegener that the continents were still moving, and he set out to explain why.

Wegener first put forward his theory of continental displacement in 1912. This proposed that, at one time, all the continents were joined to form a single landmass. He called this Pangaea, which means "all Earth" in Greek. Pangaea was surrounded by a single ocean, which he called Panthalassa, meaning "all sea." Wegener said that, starting about 300 million years ago, the supercontinent of Pangaea gradually broke apart.

EXTENSION ACTIVITY

Video

Alfred Wegener and the Continental Drift

Review Alfred Wegener's theory of continental drift by watching this video.

1. What was the general response to Wegener's theory? Why might people have responded this way? Formulate some theories and defend them with evidence.
2. What information was missing to complete Wegener's theory? Who discovered the missing information? How was this information discovered?
3. Compose a list of other scientists who saw their theories validated by later discoveries. What do they have in common?

Weblink

New Theory on Moon Formation Explained

Assess a recent theory about Moon formation.

1. Why are modern scientists not yet able to explain how the Moon was formed? What are some earlier theories of the Moon's formation? Research online or at the library to develop a response.
2. What is the Giant Impact theory? How does the new Moon formation theory differ from it? Describe it in your own words.

RUBRIC

Analyzing a Scientific Biography

Students will research the life of a scientific figure and present their findings. An exemplary biographical analysis will meet the following criteria.

- Illustrates strong knowledge of the subject
- Identifies the author of the biography
- Describes why the subject of the biography is important
- Contains information about the time and place in which the subject was born
- Lists important events in the subject's life
- Explains how events in the subject's life impacted him or her
- Makes inferences about the subject, based on events in his or her life
- Explains how the subject influenced the world while he or she lived
- Researches the cultural and historical context of the subject's life
- Examines the effect that the subject has had on the modern world
- Supplements information from the biography with independent research
- Organizes the analysis in a logical, effective manner
- Uses correct spelling, grammar, and punctuation
- Cites all sources used in the analysis

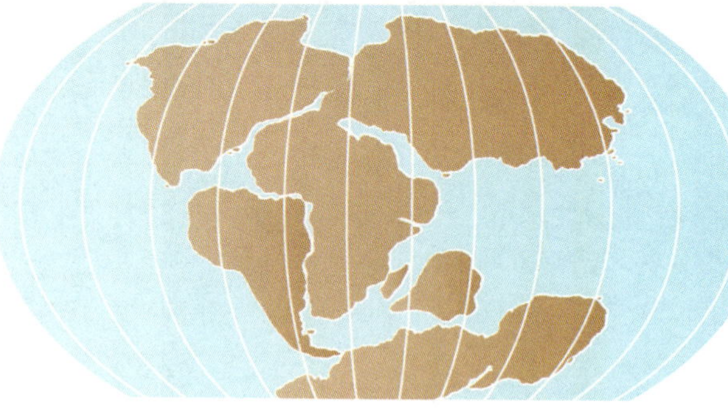

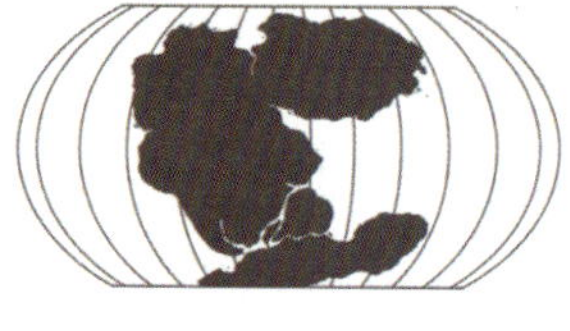

Various models have been suggested as to the way in which an original "supercontinent" might have split into the continents that exist today.

Pangaea's sections floated away on a bed of molten rock until they reached the positions they occupy now. South America and Africa began to separate around 150 million years ago, and Australia and Antarctica separated about 40 million years ago. Wegener did not know how this might have occurred, but thought tidal forces might have been involved.

In 1912, Wegener married Else Köppen, the daughter of the German meteorologist Wladimir Peter Köppen. The following year, Wegener returned to Greenland. Members of his 1913–1914 expedition covered 750 miles (1,207 km) in the longest crossing of the ice cap that had ever been made on foot. They were the first people to spend winter on the ice cap.

Wegener was wounded in World War I (1914–1918). While recovering in hospital, he wrote down his ideas about the moving continents, or "continental drift," and in 1915, he published *The Origin of Continents and Oceans*. The book received a hostile reception from geologists. This, along with the war, delayed its translation into English until 1924. The main problem was that Wegener was unable to explain how the continents moved.

Wegener's calculations of how fast the continents moved were based on faulty measurements. Other measurements implied there had been no movement of the continents, but more accurate measurements later in the twentieth century show that the continents are moving, but at about one-tenth of the speed Wegener estimated. Perhaps because of the controversy about his book, Wegener was unable to obtain a university professorship after the war. The University of Graz, in Austria, finally made him professor of meteorology and geophysics in 1924.

Wegener died during a final expedition to Greenland in 1930 and was buried by his colleague, Rasmus Villumsen, who later went missing on the journey.

Drifting Continents

During the 1920s, some geologists began to reconsider Wegener's ideas. South African geologist Alexander Logie du Toit reckoned that instead of Pangaea, two supercontinents, Laurasia and Gondwanaland, had broken apart into the continents. Like Wegener, he could not provide any explanation as to how the continents moved around the globe. Further support for Wegener's views came when the German-American geophysicist Beno Gutenberg demonstrated that it would be possible for convection currents to displace the rock beneath Earth's crust sufficiently for continents to move. The English geologist Arthur Holmes, an expert on radioactivity, showed that the radioactive decay of elements in the mantle could generate enough heat to drive the convection currents.

ALEXANDER LOGIE DU TOIT

Alexander Logie du Toit was born in Cape Town, in South Africa. He studied geology at the University of Cape Town, as well as at educational institutions in Britain. After 17 years mapping South Africa, du Toit went to South America in 1923, where he noticed similarities between the rocks of South America and Africa. He described these in *A Geological Comparison of South America and South Africa* (1927), suggesting that the two continents might once have been joined. In *Our Wandering Continents: an Hypothesis of Continental Drift* (1937), du Toit proposed that the continents of the Southern Hemisphere had once been joined in a single supercontinent that he called Gondwanaland, and that the continents of the Northern Hemisphere formed a supercontinent called Laurasia before splitting into Eur-America and Angara. This theory is now generally accepted.

EXTENSION ACTIVITY

More

The Final Trip to Greenland

Analyze the description of Wegener's last expedition to Greenland.

1. Would a scientific expedition during such extreme conditions be carried out today? Why or why not?
2. In your opinion, why did Wegener, Lowe, and Villumsen carry out the expedition despite the lack of supplies and the defection of the expedition's other members? Discuss some possible reasons.

Weblink

The Life of Beno Gutenberg

Review the scientific achievements of Beno Gutenberg by reading the text about his life and discoveries.

1. How are meteorology and Earth geophysics related? Which study of Beno Gutenberg combined these two disciplines? How did this study combine them?
2. Which sections of Earth's interior are named after Beno Gutenberg? Why are they named after him? Support your response with online research.

EDWIN HUBBLE

1889–1953

U.S. astronomer Edwin Hubble showed that there are billions of star systems outside the Milky Way Galaxy. He discovered that these distant galaxies are moving away. The farther away they are, the faster they are moving.

Edwin Hubble was born in Marshfield, Missouri. He graduated from the University of Chicago in 1910 and then studied law at Oxford University, England. Back in the United States, he worked for a law practice before going to study a PhD in astronomy at the Yerkes Observatory in Wisconsin. After serving in World War I (1914–1918), he joined the Mount Wilson Observatory in Pasadena, California, where he stayed for the rest of his career.

At the time, a major argument was raging about the size and structure of the universe. U.S. astronomer Harlow Shapley, at the Mount Wilson Observatory, asserted that the Milky Way, Earth's galaxy, more or less made up the whole of the universe. The U.S. astronomer Henrietta Leavitt had discovered a type of star called a cepheid variable, which provided a key to measure very large distances in space. Shapley used Leavitt's discovery to map the galaxy. He calculated the relative distances of star clusters containing cepheid variables from Earth and from each other. His calculations were inaccurate, because he was unaware that gases and dust between stars absorb light and affect brightness, or magnitude. The diameter of the galaxy was later revised downward to about 100,000 light-years.

In 1920, Shapley held a debate with U.S. astronomer Heber Curtis about nebulae. Today, astronomers use the term "nebula" to describe interstellar clouds of gas or dust, but before powerful telescopes, any fuzzy celestial object was called a nebula. Some were clouds of dust, but Curtis asserted that other spiral nebulae lay outside the Milky Way.

The Mount Wilson Observatory was originally built by U.S. astronomer George Ellery Hale in 1904.

One was the Andromeda nebula, a spiral-shaped cluster. Curtis estimated its distance from Earth to be about 500,000 light-years. He believed spiral nebulae were independent star systems "comparable with our own galaxy in dimension and in number of component units." Shapley disagreed. He thought spiral nebulae lay inside the galaxy.

In 1923, using the 100-inch (2.5-m) telescope at Mount Wilson Observatory, Hubble made his first major astronomical discovery. He focused on Andromeda and resolved the outer region of the nebula into individual stars, including some giant cepheid stars. Using these as markers, Hubble calculated that Andromeda is about 1 million light-years away, and therefore far outside Earth's galaxy. This confirmed Curtis's theory, although Hubble's estimate was too low. Between 1925 and 1929, Hubble demonstrated that spiral nebulae lie enormous distances outside Earth's galaxy. They are isolated star systems. Hubble suggested that Earth's galaxy is the largest in the universe. In fact, scientists know now that it is an average-size spiral galaxy.

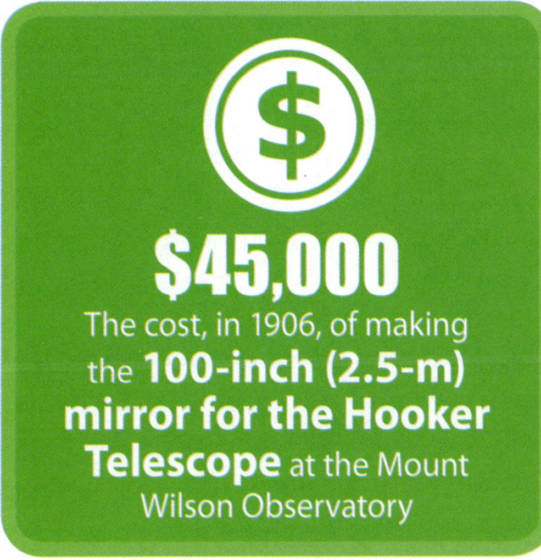

EXTENSION ACTIVITY

More

George Ellery Hale

Assess the scientific achievements of George Ellery Hale.

1. Why are telescopes important for astronomical research? How did Hale spur the development of this scientific discipline with his work? Research and describe Hale's contribution to astronomy.
2. In your opinion, why has George Ellery Hale not become a famous name outside scientific circles? Suggest and evaluate some possible reasons.

Document

Photographic Investigations of Faint Nebulae

Analyze the first page of Edwin Hubble's dissertation, published in 1920.

1. To which public is this text addressed? What elements of the text could allow you to determine that? How does Hubble describe the purpose of his study?
2. According to Hubble, what is the study of nebulae? What are nebulae? What knowledge of them did scientists have at the time this text was published?

RUBRIC

Answer a Scientific Question

Students will define a scientific question or problem, and carry out an investigation or experiment to answer it, then write a report on their findings. An exemplary report will meet the following criteria.

- Problem is written in the form of a question with a question mark at the end
- Hypothesis is written as a guess or explanation to the answer of the problem
- Hypothesis is written in a complete sentence (for example, "I think ...," "I hypothesize ...," "If..., then...")
- Variable and controls are clearly identified
- Procedure steps are in numbered order
- Procedure steps show what to measure and where to record the data
- Procedure steps are written in complete sentences
- Data is organized in a data table
- The investigation or experiment includes more then one trial
- All numbers have labels
- All calculations are complete
- Conclusion is written in complete sentences
- Conclusion states whether the hypothesis was right or wrong
- Conclusion answers the question written in the problem

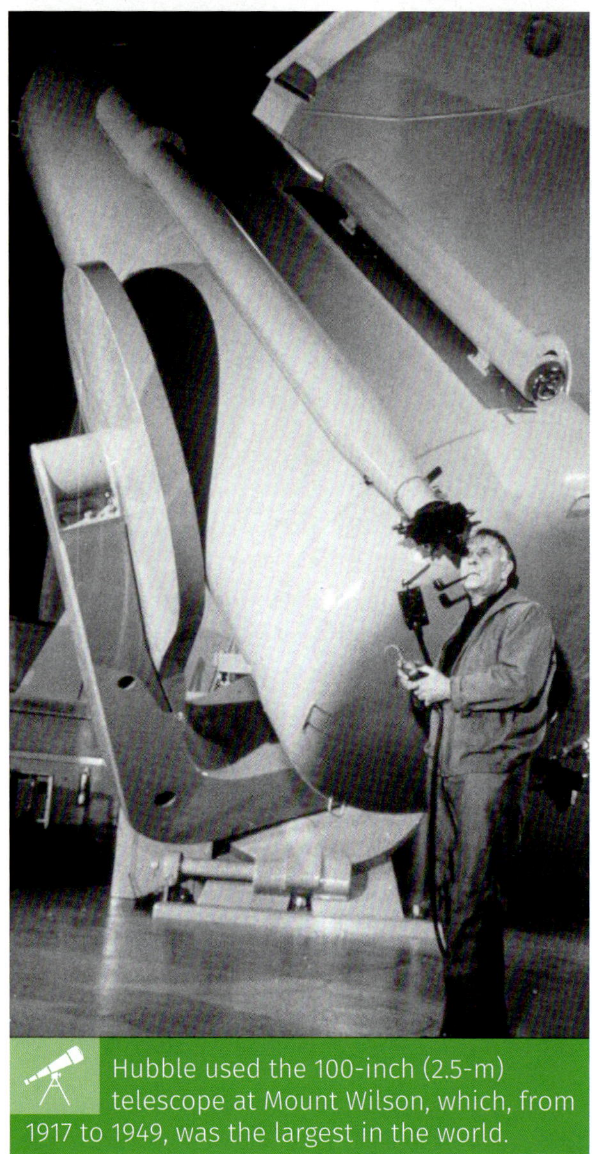

Hubble used the 100-inch (2.5-m) telescope at Mount Wilson, which, from 1917 to 1949, was the largest in the world.

Fast-Moving Stars

While exploring these outer galaxies, Hubble made a second major discovery. He found that they seem to be moving away from Earth's galaxy, and that the farther away they are, the faster they are moving. Hubble proved this by studying the **redshift** of various galaxies. Redshift is a phenomenon in which a wavelength changes because of relative motion between the source of the wavelength and an observer.

Light travels in waves, and different frequencies of light waves correspond to different colors. At one end of the scale, lower-frequency waves produce the color red, while at the other end of the scale, higher-frequency waves produce the color blue. Light waves moving toward Earth are compressed, have a higher frequency, and so shift toward the blue end of the scale. Light traveling away from an observer will spread out and have a lower frequency, so its wavelengths shift toward the red end of the scale. The faster the light-emitting objects are receding, the greater the shift to red.

By 1929, Hubble noticed that the more distant the galaxy, the greater its redshift. That is how he concluded that galaxies are moving away from one another. He then showed that their speed increases proportionately with their distance from Earth. A galaxy twice as far away will have twice the redshift, and a galaxy 10 times farther away will have 10 times the redshift. This is now known as Hubble's law.

Hubble examined many galaxies between 1928 and 1936. The relationship between distance and redshift held true. Scientists suspected that galaxies are moving away from Earth because the universe is expanding. What is happening can be explained by imagining dots drawn on a partially inflated balloon. The dots represent other galaxies. As the balloon is inflated, so it expands, making the dots move farther apart from one another.

From his observations, Hubble identified three types of galaxies by their shape. The main shapes were elliptical, spiral, and bar, or barred spiral, and each had subtypes. Some astronomers used the different shapes of galaxy to produce theories about the way in which galaxies may have evolved.

The Sombrero Galaxy is an elliptical galaxy 31 million light-years from Earth in the constellation of Virgo. It is about one-third the size of the Milky Way.

They suggested that ellipticals developed naturally into spirals, although it is now thought that spirals merge to form ellipticals.

Hubble's work with the telescope at Mount Wilson made him a public success. He relished such attention, but his prolonged absences and overseas tours damaged his reputation with his colleagues and other astronomers. When the directorship of the laboratory became vacant in 1945, Hubble, the obvious choice, was passed over in favor of Ira Bowen. Hubble died in California on September 28, 1953.

FRED HOYLE

The astronomer and mathematician Fred Hoyle was born in Yorkshire, England, in 1915. He studied at Cambridge University, England, where, in 1958, he became professor of astronomy and experimental philosophy. In 1948, with British **cosmologist** Hermann Bondi and Austrian-born astronomer Thomas Gold, Hoyle proposed the "steady state" theory of the origin of the universe. This alternative model to the **big-bang theory** suggested that the universe had always existed in its present form, and that new matter was constantly being created to sustain its density. Although the steady-state theory is no longer widely accepted, Hoyle went on to formulate other theories on the origins of stars and elements within them. From 1972 to 1978, Hoyle was professor-at-large at Cornell University, Ithaca, New York. He was the author of many books on scientific subjects, including works of science fiction. He died in 2001.

EXTENSION ACTIVITY

More

An Expanding Universe

Examine the evolution of the theory of an expanding universe.

1. What is the big-bang theory? How is this theory linked to the idea of an expanding universe? Explain the two theories and their connection in your own words.
2. What do the expressions "matter with no motion" and "motion with no matter" mean? Research online to learn their meanings. Then, compare and contrast them.

Weblink

Mount Wilson Observatory Virtual Tour

Explore the interior of Mount Wilson Observatory.

1. How is the structure of Mount Wilson Observatory organized? Does this organization respond to any scientific need? Formulate some hypotheses.
2. What equipment can be seen in Mount Wilson Observatory? How does this equipment function? Use internet research to assist in the formulation of a response.

LINUS PAULING

1901–1994

Linus Pauling was born in Portland, Oregon. In 1917, he enrolled at Oregon Agricultural College to study chemical engineering. After graduating, he went on to the California Institute of Technology in Pasadena, where he gained his doctorate in 1925. Pauling then worked with European physicists such as Niels Bohr, who had proposed a quantum model of the atom, and Erwin Schrödinger, the Austrian physicist involved in developing the new quantum mechanics. This branch of mechanics governed the behavior of small-scale physical phenomena such as atoms and electrons. Back in the United States, Pauling began to apply the principles of quantum mechanics to his work on the structure of molecules.

In a career spanning many branches of science, Linus Pauling is best remembered for his work on the structure of molecules and **chemical bonds**. In 1954, he was awarded the Nobel Prize in Chemistry. He also carried out important research into proteins and blood.

U.S. chemist Gilbert Lewis suggested in 1916 that atoms bond by sharing electrons. He added data about electrons to the periodic table.

Structure of Chemical Bonds

Molecules are the smallest unit of a chemical compound. The links that hold molecules together are known as chemical bonds. Electrons govern how atoms react, or bond, with other atoms to form a molecule. Atoms seek chemical stability. Those with a full outer shell of electrons are stable, but those with an incomplete outer shell of electrons try to join up with other atoms.

Atoms combine by transfer of electrons from one atom to the other, a process called ionic bonding, or by sharing one electron from each atom so that both electrons orbit around both nuclei, which is known as covalent bonding. An example of a covalent bond is the H^2 molecule. Hydrogen is the lightest atom. It has a positively charged nucleus, a proton, orbited by a negatively charged electron in its outer shell. It can form a more stable structure by joining with a second hydrogen atom to share a pair of electrons.

When an atom loses or gains electrons by joining with another atom, it becomes electrically charged and is known as an ion. An ionic compound is formed when ions with opposite charges are held together by electrical attraction. The ions form a regular array, or crystal.

Sodium chloride (NaCl), common table salt, is a compound of sodium and chlorine. Sodium (Na°) and chlorine (Cl°) atoms are neutral. The sign ° indicates that they carry no charge. Sodium's outer shell contains a single electron, however, meaning that it is it very reactive chemically. In contrast, chlorine's outer shell has seven electrons, one short of the eight electrons favored for a stable atom. If a chlorine atom meets a sodium atom, the sodium atom loses an electron to become a positive ion (Na+). Meanwhile, the chlorine gains an electron to become a negative ion (Cl-) and forms a sodium chloride crystal.

A crystal of sodium chloride, or table salt, is formed by a regular framework of positive sodium ions and negative chlorine ions.

Pauling's research into the interactions among electrons in forming molecules built on the work of the U.S. chemist Gilbert Lewis, who first came up with the idea that chemical bonds were formed by sharing and transferring electrons. Pauling applied the ideas of quantum mechanics to his research. Quantum theory suggested that electrons have spin and that their motion is wavelike.

Pauling said that molecules might alternate or "resonate" between the two states. Molecules form single, double, or triple bonds. Pauling brought together his theories in his book *The Nature of the Chemical Bond, and the Structure of Molecules and Crystals* (1939).

EXTENSION ACTIVITY

 **More**

Gilbert Newton Lewis and Dorothy Hodgkin

Review the scientific discoveries of Gilbert Newton Lewis and Dorothy Hodgkin and research online for further information about them.

1. What is an "acid"? What is a "base"? How are they important to the understanding of molecules and their function?
2. How are penicillin, vitamin B12, and insulin used? What are possible applications of Hodgkin's discoveries about these substances?

 **Weblink**

Chemical Investigations as a Teenager

Analyze Linus Pauling's early approach to scientific research.

1. Why did Linus Pauling tell this anecdote? What kind of information does such anecdote provide about him?
2. Why did Pauling not rely on reading? Why did he favor empiric observation? How did his attitude evolve over time? Support your answers with excerpts from Pauling's anecdote.

EXTENSION ACTIVITY

Analyzing Lectures as Arguments

Students will analyze a lecture as an argument and write a response. An exemplary analysis will meet the following criteria.

- Presents a strong thesis that is based on analysis of the argument presented in the lecture and how the argument is presented
- Consistently uses strong textual evidence to support the thesis
- Presents an engaging and effective introduction, body, and conclusion
- Structures the analysis in a logical order
- Develops a thorough analysis of the lecture
- Identifies the main points presented in the lecture
- Identifies the speaker and infers how his or her life may have shaped this argument
- Identifies when and where the lecture was given
- Determines the lecture's intended audience
- Uses strong evidence from the lecture to show how the speaker supports his or her argument
- Analyzes the language used to convey the lecture's argument
- Demonstrates understanding of the historical and societal context in which the lecture was given and connects that context to the speaker's argument
- Properly integrates quotations
- Properly cites all sources used

Building Blocks of Life

In the mid-1930s, Pauling began investigating the molecules of living organisms. He started by studying proteins. These are large molecules that play an essential role in the life processes of all living organisms. The building blocks of proteins are amino acids, a group of compounds that can form long chains, or polymers, joined by linkages called peptide bonds. Pauling worked out that certain proteins have helical structures. In fact, he was close to unraveling the secret behind the structure of DNA, the long chain molecule that carries genetic information. In 1953, in England, the American James Watson and Englishman Francis Crick found that DNA is made up of two chains twisted around each other to form a double helix.

Understanding Sickle-Cell Anemia

Pauling also investigated the hemoglobin molecule. This is what gives red blood cells their color. In the 1940s, Pauling studied the blood disorder sickle-cell anemia. Normal red blood cells have the shape of flattened disks. Cells with sickle-cell anemia are elongated crescents. As a result, these distorted blood cells can block smaller blood vessels, causing tissue destruction. Pauling thought the illness arose from a difference in a vital molecule in the patient. Hemoglobin binds with oxygen and carries it to all parts of the body. Pauling knew that sickle cells appear more frequently in deoxygenated blood, which has already distributed oxygen to the body and is returning to the heart through the veins. He concluded, therefore, that the formation of sickle cells was probably related to the way in which the hemoglobin molecule binds to oxygen.

Research by U.S. chemist Charles Coryell in 1935 had established that hemoglobin atoms have weak positive magnetism. The hemoglobin in arteries, which is full of oxygen, has weak negative magnetism. Pauling reasoned that if the hemoglobin molecule contained unpaired electrons, giving it an electrical charge, the strength of the charge might alter the shape of the red blood cells from a flat disk to a sickle.

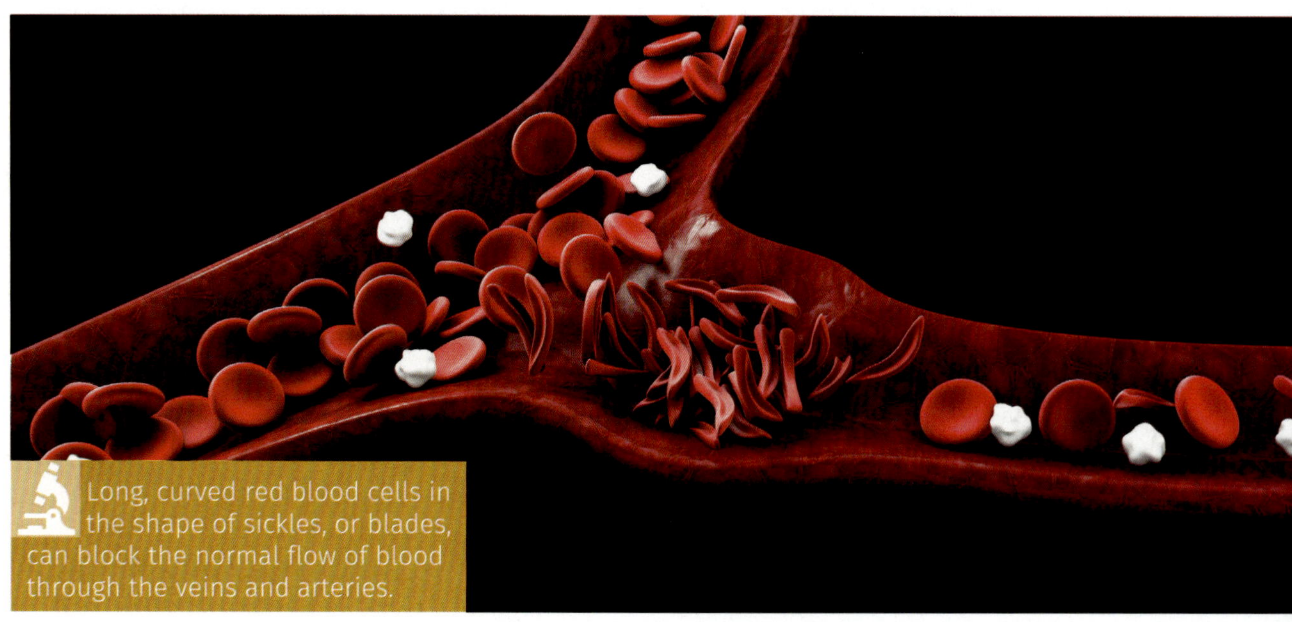

Long, curved red blood cells in the shape of sickles, or blades, can block the normal flow of blood through the veins and arteries.

A PERSONAL QUEST

In 1970, Linus Pauling published a book supporting the idea that large, regular doses of vitamin C could prevent people from getting colds. In 1971, he claimed that, with such doses, "the mortality from cancer could be reduced by 10 percent." There was much hostility to Pauling's ideas from other scientists, and trials at the Mayo clinic in 1979 concluded that cancer patients given high-dose vitamin C did no better than those given only a placebo, or fake pill. Pauling dismissed the trials and pursued his research at his own Linus Pauling Institute for Science and Medicine, set up in 1973. In 1985, another study disproved Pauling's claims, as have other studies since. Vitamin C has many benefits, but there is no proof that high doses of the vitamin prevent illness. In fact, taking very large amounts can actually be harmful. However, Pauling convinced many people that taking extra vitamin C is vital to their health, helping to create a multi-million-dollar industry in vitamin supplements.

By 1948, Pauling had confirmed his theory. Studies showed that the hemoglobin molecules of sickle-cell patients carry a higher electrical charge than ordinary hemoglobin. He had identified the first molecular disease.

Antinuclear Battles

During the 1950s, Linus Pauling became increasingly involved in the political movement against nuclear weapons. Many people even suspected him of being a communist sympathizer. In 1958, he published a book called *No More War*. That provoked a reply, *Our Nuclear Future*, from Hungarian-born U.S. physicist Edward Teller, who had helped to develop the atomic bomb and who argued the case for nuclear weapons. Undeterred, Pauling continued his protests against nuclear bomb testing. In 1962, he was given the Nobel Prize for Peace. In his last years, Pauling worked on the chemistry of the brain and its effect on mental illness, and on high temperature superconductivity. He died of prostate cancer in California in August 1994, aged 93.

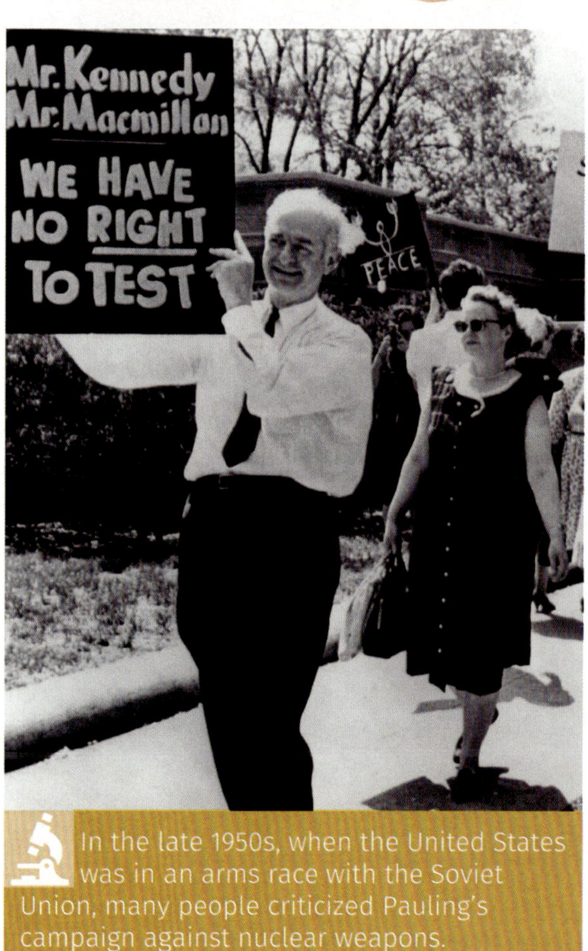

In the late 1950s, when the United States was in an arms race with the Soviet Union, many people criticized Pauling's campaign against nuclear weapons.

EXTENSION ACTIVITY

Document

Nobel Lecture

Analyze the text of the lecture Linus Pauling gave in 1954 after being awarded the Nobel Prize for Chemistry.

1. Why was Linus Pauling awarded the Nobel Prize? What is the main topic of Pauling's Nobel lecture? In your opinion, why did he choose to present this topic? Discuss some possible reasons.
2. Is this text addressed to specialists or to non-specialists in Chemistry? Why? According to the lecture's conclusion, what were Pauling's predictions for the future of chemistry? Was Pauling right in his prediction? Support your answer by researching online.

Video

No More War — Nobel Laureate Dr. Linus Pauling

Evaluate Linus Pauling's opinion of the atomic bomb, expressed during the commemoration for the sixteenth anniversary of the atomic bomb explosion in Hiroshima.

1. Why did Linus Pauling define the atomic bomb as the "ultimate immorality"? Do you agree with him? Why or why not? Defend your idea.
2. In what year did Pauling express this opinion? What could have influenced his vision of the atomic bomb? Would he have a different opinion, had he lived in a different historical period? Formulate some hypotheses.

STEPHEN HAWKING

1942–2018

Diagnosed with a wasting disease at the age of 20, Stephen Hawking overcame his affliction. He became one of the best-known of all scientists. Much of his work centered on **black holes**, and on the dynamics of relativity and quantum theory. He was also a best-selling author.

Stephen Hawking was born in Oxford, England, on January 8, 1942. In 1959, he enrolled at Oxford University to study mathematics and physics. However, he found the work tedious and did little studying. He chose only the theoretical physics questions in his final exam papers. After a further oral test, he graduated with high honors. In 1962, Hawking enrolled at the University of Cambridge to pursue a PhD in cosmology, the study of the universe. However, in 1963, he was diagnosed with motor neuron disease, which causes muscular wasting and eventually death. At the age of 21, he was given two years to live. The news plunged him into a depression. Gradually, however, he returned to his work. The disease leaves the mind unaffected. As long as he could think, then he could carry on. Hawking then got engaged, the disease stabilized, and he began to regain enthusiasm for life and work.

Life History of Stars

Hawking had become interested in the ideas of the mathematician Roger Penrose, who was studying collapsed stars now known as black holes.
The lifespan of a star depends on its mass and luminosity, or brightness. A typical star begins as a gas cloud, mainly of hydrogen. The cloud contracts, and gas atoms hit each other faster and more frequently. This heats the gas, and some of the atoms fuse to form helium. This "nuclear fusion" makes the star hot, while the released energy produces enough outward pressure to support the star's atoms against its own **gravity**. Eventually, the star stops contracting, but the conversion of hydrogen into helium makes it continue to shine.

When all the hydrogen in the star's core has been converted into helium, the core contracts because it no longer generates enough outward pressure to counteract its gravitational attraction. The contraction heats up the core and forces the outer layers outward, so that the star expands for some 100 to 200 million years, becoming a "red giant" star. Its later history depends on its initial mass. A star with less than 1.5 times the Sun's mass becomes a "white dwarf." Any star that has more than 1.5 **solar masses** will not become a white dwarf. This is known as the Chandrasekhar limit.

Anatomy of a Black Hole

Penrose had been schooled in two key theories. The first was the general theory of relativity formulated in 1915 by Albert Einstein, which governed gravity and larger structures of the universe. The second was quantum theory, which dealt with small-scale interactions, light, and **radiation**.

Einstein's theory predicted that an object that had a mass more than three times that of the Sun would collapse in on itself so much that it would bend space-time around itself. Light rays near such an object would be deflected so much that photons, which are bundles of **electromagnetic** energy associated with light, would orbit the star's center. Not even light would escape. The result would be a dark star, later named a "black hole." However, scientists did not believe anything more dense than a white dwarf existed.

Quantum theory suggested that stars could collapse beyond the white dwarf stage. The atom's nucleus is formed of protons and neutrons. Each nucleus is surrounded by electrons, with a negative charge. If a star of more than 1.2 solar masses was compressed, the electrons would be forced into the nucleus, merge with the protons, and produce neutrons. The result would be a neutron star.

The intense gravity of a black hole pulls in everything that surrounds it—even light.

EXTENSION ACTIVITY

More

A Brief History of Time

Review the story of the publication of *A Brief History of Time*.

1. Why did *A Brief History of Time* strike such a chord with the general public? Justify your answer with evidence.
2. If you have not read the book, research its content online. What is the concept of time according to the book? How does this concept of time differ from the general idea of time held by non-specialists? Why?

Weblink

Stephen Hawking Is Still Underrated

Analyze Stephen Hawking's discoveries on particles.

1. What is the physicists definition of the word "real"? How does it differ from the common meaning of this word? How is it similar? Answer providing examples.
2. What did Hawking discover about particles? Explain it in your own words.
3. How did Hawking's disability affect his research? How did it stimulate his research? Would Hawking's discoveries have been possible, had his personal condition been different? Defend your position with reasoning and evidence.

RUBRIC

Analyzing a Magazine Article

Students will assess a magazine article and write an analysis. An exemplary analysis will meet the following criteria.

- Identifies the topic of the article
- Identifies the main points and opinions presented in the article
- Identifies the writer of the article
- Presents information about the writer and infers how his or her life may have shaped this opinion
- Assesses the writer's reliability
- Analyzes how the writer makes his or her argument
- Uses evidence from the article to show how the writer supports his or her argument
- Analyzes the writer's use of literary devices to enhance the article
- Differentiates between the facts and opinions presented in the article
- Identifies when and where the article was published, and determines its intended audience
- Identifies and understands the goals of the article
- Assesses the effectiveness of the format in presenting the writer's argument
- Connects the article to the societal and historical context in which it was written
- Infers what is not said about this topic in the article
- Identifies what information is unintentionally implied in the article

CREATION OF A SINGULARITY

Roger Penrose showed that, if the remnant of a neutron star was more than three solar masses, it would collapse beyond the white dwarf stage, crushing its neutrons and creating a black hole. Penrose showed that the star would reach a singularity, a state in which the star reaches a point of infinite density and zero volume. In this singularity, general relativity would break down and time would end. The process begins with a star collapsing under its own gravitational pressure. The star's explosion inward makes an indentation on the surrounding space. Nothing can escape from the event horizon this creates.

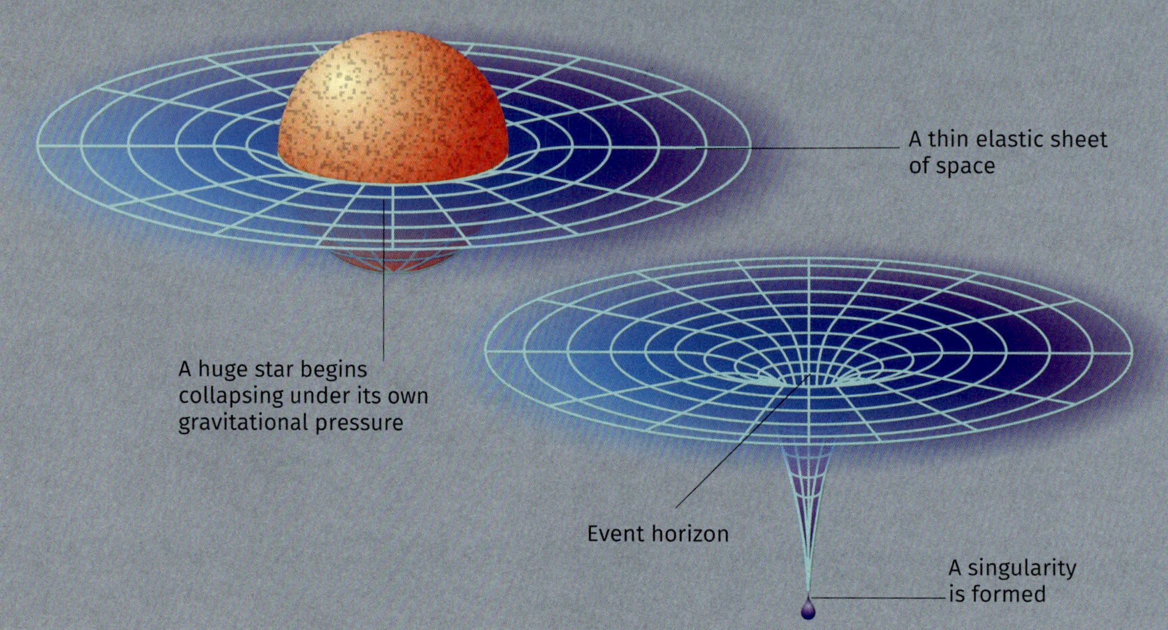

A tiny neutron star could have a density several million times more than that of a white dwarf. A large star would collapse further still. It would reach a point of zero volume and infinite density that Penrose called a "singularity."

Hawking earned his doctorate by applying Penrose's singularity theory to the universe. Soon afterward, he began to work with Penrose. Both men accepted the theory that the universe emerged from an extremely hot, dense state, the "big bang," and was still expanding. In 1970, Penrose and Hawking stated that, "provided that general relativity is correct and the universe contains as much matter as we observe," there must have been a singularity at the time of the big bang. The big bang singularity was a beginning of time. Anything that might have existed before could not be considered part of the universe.

While a black hole reaches a singularity at the end of its life cycle, Penrose and Hawking argued that the expanding universe must also have begun with a singularity. This suggested that the expansion of the universe from the point of the big bang singularity must be the reverse of the process that creates a black hole. The universe was like a black hole, but inside out.

New Theories about the Universe

A black hole can be formed from any object, if it is squeezed into a small enough volume. Hawking argued that a pressure great enough to compress matter in this way existed after the big bang, and could have created mini black holes, even as small as a proton. Hawking used quantum theory to support his argument. According to quantum theory, every charged particle has an antiparticle. A negatively charged electron has a positively charged positron. On meeting, these opposite charges destroy each other, creating energy.

Quantum theory claims that space is rich in pairs such as electrons and positrons and other virtual pairs that destroy each other and reform from the released energy. Suppose, Hawking argued, a virtual pair is near a black hole. One particle could be captured by the black hole, leaving its partner to escape. To an observer, it would appear that the black hole was emitting what is now called Hawking Radiation. Hawking Radiation would drain energy from the black hole. Eventually, it would lose all its energy, and therefore its mass, and disappear. The mini black holes would explode.

Hawking argued that, if the laws of physics could break down at the start of the universe, they could break down anywhere. He developed the No Boundary Proposal. This removes the singularity at the beginning of the universe. In the big bang theory, the universe expands from the singularity. It then collapses back to a singularity in "the big crunch." This model creates "edges" in time in the singularities at the start and end of the universe. The No Boundary Proposal suggested that time and space together form a surface that was finite in size but had no boundary. This can be imagined by picturing the expanding universe as a globe. The big bang can be seen as a point, such as the North Pole on Earth. Drawing a circle around that point, like a line of latitude on the globe, defines the universe. Over time, the lines of latitude move away from the North Pole. This is the universe expanding. Eventually, it reaches its widest point, or equator. The lines of latitude become smaller again, until the universe contracts to a point, in this case, at the South Pole.

Hawking's proposal removed the idea of an "edge" in time. If someone walks from the North Pole, they do not fall off the world. From the North Pole every direction is south. In the same way, Hawking's theory meant that, from the big bang, every time was in the future. The universe had no beginning or end, it just "was." Stephen Hawking died on March 14, 2018, aged 76.

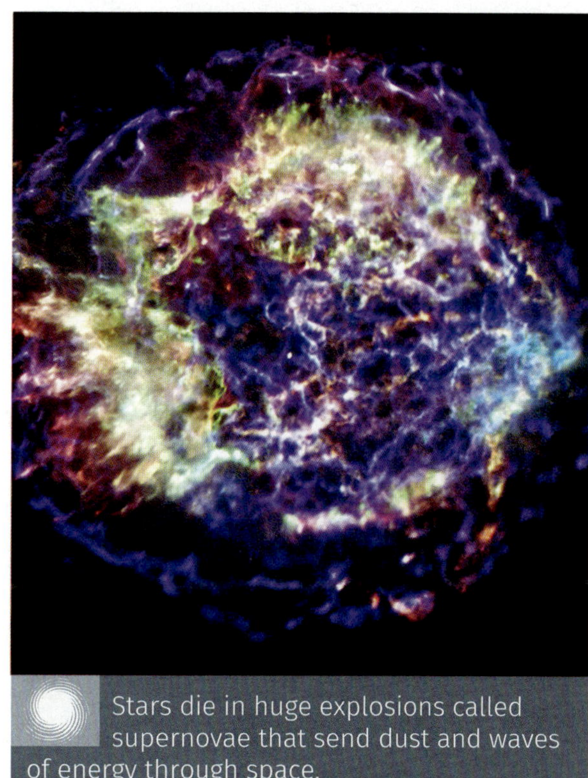

Stars die in huge explosions called supernovae that send dust and waves of energy through space.

EXTENSION ACTIVITY

More

The Grand Unifying Theory

Analyze the concept of the theory of everything.

1. Compare the theory of relativity and quantum theory. Why is it necessary to reconcile them according to scientists? What would the implications of a theory of everything be in everyday life? Use research to discover more information, then, formulate a defensible response.
2. Why did Stephen Hawking believe that this theory will make ordinary people able to discuss the reason for the universe's existence?

Weblink

Stephen Hawking, Pop Culture Icon

Review how Stephen Hawking became part of pop culture.

1. What might the consequences of popularity be on Hawking's scientific career? Why? Justify your ideas.
2. In your opinion, why did Stephen Hawking take part in non-scientific public events? Theorize and defend possible reasons.

RUBRIC

Creating a Timeline

Students will explore a topic related to a scientific event and create a timeline to present their research on scientific events connected to this topic. An exemplary timeline will meet the following criteria.

- Includes the most significant events pertaining to the topic to be compared and analyzed
- Includes interesting events
- Uses accurate information for all events, including date, location, and major details
- Orders the events in a chronological sequence
- Describes each event with accurate, vivid, and specific details
- Presents the topic from three or more perspectives
- Inspires the reader to ask thoughtful questions regarding the events and perspectives presented in the timeline
- Uses correct spelling, grammar, and punctuation
- Presents the timeline in a visually attractive and striking manner
- Presents the timeline in a neat, organized manner that is logical and easy to follow
- Uses creativity to present the timeline in an engaging manner
- Effectively communicates historical information relating to the topic
- Supports each event with reliable sources
- Includes a correctly formatted bibliography of all sources used to create the timeline

Timeline of Scientific Breakthroughs

The history of chemistry, Earth, and space science has been marked by important breakthroughs. Scientists have pieced together information about the physical building blocks that make up Earth and space, and identified Earth's place in the universe. Their investigations have revealed that the same rules that govern tiny particles might hold clues to the structures of the universe.

1543 — On his deathbed, Nicolaus Copernicus receives a copy of his book proposing that Earth orbits the Sun.

1609 — Galileo Galilei builds an improved version of the telescope. In 1610, he uses the new device to discover the moons of Jupiter, sunspots, and the jagged surface of the Moon.

1778–1779 — Antoine Lavoisier identifies and names oxygen, and describes its role in combustion. He later goes on to identify hydrogen.

1869 — Dmitri Mendeleev formulates periodic law and arranges the elements in a periodic table.

1912 — Alfred Wegener proposes that Earth's continents were once all joined together and have become separated by a process he calls "continental drift."

1923 — Edwin Hubble realizes that spiral nebulae are star systems that lie far beyond the Milky Way Galaxy.

1939 — Linus Pauling publishes his theories and descriptions of chemical bonds between atoms in compounds.

1970 — Stephen Hawking and Roger Penrose suggest that the Big Bang started with a singularity.

Quiz

1 Which ancient Greek thinker suggested Earth circles the Sun centuries before Nicolaus Copernicus?

2 Where did Galileo Galilei test his theory that falling bodies travel at the same speed, despite their relative size?

3 In what way did Copernicus and Galileo contradict the teachings of the Catholic Church about the universe?

4 Which two British chemists made valuable contributions to Antoine Lavoisier's work on gases?

5 What was the name of the huge work Alexander von Humboldt spent the last 20 years of his life writing?

6 How many rows did Dmitri Mendeleev include in his original periodic table of the elements?

7 What name did Alfred Wegener gave to the landmass of which he suggested all the continents were once part?

8 What sort of stars did Edwin Hubble use as the markers to calculate the distance to the Andromeda galaxy?

9 What blood disorder did Linus Pauling investigate in the 1940s?

10 Which British scientist's singularity theory did Stephen Hawking apply to the whole universe?

ANSWERS

1. Aristarchus of Samos 2. The Leaning Tower of Pisa
3. The Church taught that Earth was the center of the universe
4. Joseph Priestley and Henry Cavendish 5. *Cosmos* 6. Seven
7. Pangaea 8. Cepheid variables 9. Sickle-cell anemia
10. Roger Penrose

EXTENSION ACTIVITY

Transparency–Timeline

Timeline of Scientific Breakthroughs

Analyze important events and advancements in the fields of chemistry, Earth, and space science in different cultural, historical, and contemporary contexts.

1. Why might these events be featured in the timeline? What makes these events important or significant?
2. How might people from different social or ideological groups have interpreted these events when they took place? How might their opinions differ from those of people in the same social or ideological groups today? Why?
3. What effects did one of these scientific breakthroughs have on modern science?
4. How might these events have shaped the world today? Explain your response with evidence found on the internet or at the library.
5. How might recent events affect the way people interpret these past events?

Key Words

alchemists: early scientists who tried to turn substances into other substances

astronomers: people who study of the universe

atmosphere: an envelope of gases around a planet

atomic number: the number of protons in an atom's nucleus

atomic weight: the mass of an atom on a scale where hydrogen has a weight of 1

atoms: tiny, indivisible particles that form all matter

big-bang theory: a theory that the universe began in a massive explosion

black holes: stars that have collapsed to become objects of zero size and infinite density

celestial: belonging to space

chemical bonds: forces of attraction that hold together atoms to form molecules

chemistry: the science concerned with elements and compounds, their makeup, and reactions between them

compound: a substance with molecules made up of atoms of more than one element

cosmologist: someone who studies the origin and evolution of the universe

earth sciences: sciences concerned with Earth, such as geology and geography

ecological: concerned with relations between living things and their environment

electromagnetic: related to how energy is transmitted

elements: substances that cannot be split chemically into simpler substances

galaxies: star systems

geography: Earth's natural features and natural resources

geology: the study of Earth's structure and composition

gravity: the force of attraction between all matter

light-years: units based on the distance traveled by light in a vacuum in one year, equal to about 5.88 trillion miles (9.46 trillion km)

magnetic field: forces surrounding a magnet or charged particle

mass: the amount of matter in an object

mathematics: the study of shape, quantity, and space

matter: anything that occupies space and has mass

nucleus: the positively charged region at the center of an atom

orbits: circular paths around a central point

periodic table: an ordered arrangement of the elements

physics: the study of matter and energy

radiation: the emission of electromagnetism or subatomic particles

redshift: a shift in spectral lines toward the red end of the spectrum

solar masses: units of mass based on the weight of the Sun

solar system: the Sun and all the celestial bodies around it

Index

LIGHTBOX

SUPPLEMENTARY RESOURCES

Click on the plus icon found in the bottom left corner of each spread to open additional teacher resources.

- Download and print the book's quizzes and activities
- Access curriculum correlations
- Explore additional web applications that enhance the Lightbox experience

LIGHTBOX DIGITAL TITLES
Packed full of integrated media

VIDEOS

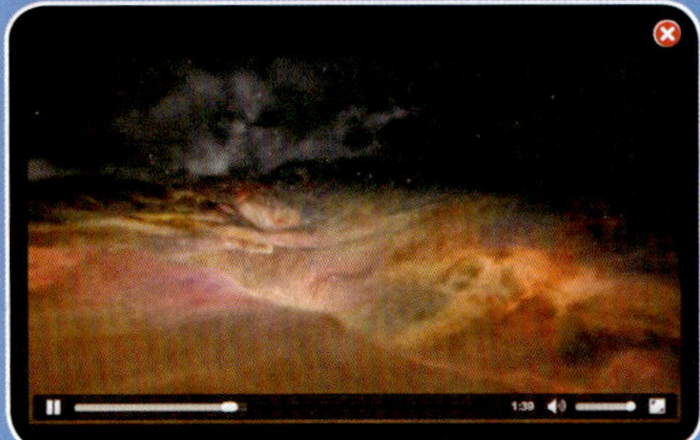

INTERACTIVE MAPS

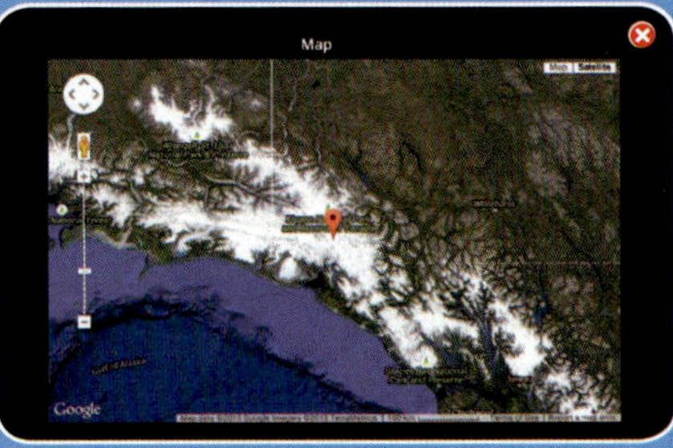

WEBLINKS

SLIDESHOWS

QUIZZES

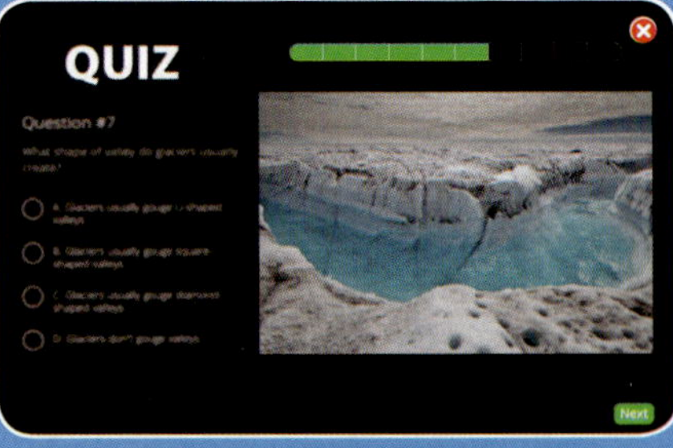

OPTIMIZED FOR
- ✓ TABLETS
- ✓ WHITEBOARDS
- ✓ COMPUTERS
- ✓ AND MUCH MORE!

Published by Smartbook Media Inc.
350 5th Avenue, 59th Floor New York, NY 10118
Website: www.openlightbox.com

Library of Congress Control Number: 2018937317

ISBN 978-1-5105-4009-5 (hardcover)
ISBN 978-1-5105-4010-1 (multi-user eBook)

Printed in Brainerd, Minnesota, United States
1 2 3 4 5 6 7 8 9 0 22 21 20 19 18

062018
121217

Project Coordinator: Jared Siemens
Designer: Ana María Vidal

Every reasonable effort has been made to trace ownership and to obtain permission to reprint copyright material. The publisher would be pleased to have any errors or omissions brought to its attention so that they may be corrected in subsequent printings. The publisher acknowledges Getty Images, Shutterstock, Newscom, iStock, and Alamy as its primary image suppliers for this title.